Monologues from Shakespeare's First Folio for Younger Men: *The Comedies*

The Applause Shakespeare Monologue Series

<u>Other Shakespeare Titles From Applause</u>

Once More unto the Speech Dear Friends
Volume One: The Comedies
Compiled and Edited with Commentary by Neil Freeman

Once More unto the Speech Dear Friends
Volume Two: The Histories
Compiled and Edited with Commentary by Neil Freeman

Once More unto the Speech Dear Friends
Volume Three: The Tragedies
Compiled and Edited with Commentary by Neil Freeman

The Applause First Folio in Modern Type
Prepared and Annotated by Neil Freeman

The Folio Texts
Prepared and Annotated by Neil Freeman, Each of the 36 plays of the
Applause First Folio in Modern Type individually bound

The Applause Shakespeare Library
Plays of Shakespeare Edited for Performance

Soliloquy: The Shakespeare Monologues

Monologues from Shakespeare's First Folio for Younger Men: *The Comedies*

Compilation and Commentary by
Neil Freeman

Edited by
Paul Sugarman

APPLAUSE
THEATRE & CINEMA BOOKS
Guilford, Connecticut

APPLAUSE
THEATRE & CINEMA BOOKS

An imprint of Globe Pequot, the trade division of
The Rowman & Littlefield Publishing Group, Inc.
4501 Forbes Blvd., Ste. 200
Lanham, MD 20706
www.rowman.com

Distributed by NATIONAL BOOK NETWORK

Library of Congress Cataloging-in-Publication Data available

Library of Congress Control Number: 2021944373

ISBN 978-1-4930-5688-0 (paperback)
ISBN 978-1-4930-5689-7 (ebook)

∞™ The paper used in this publication meets the minimum requirements of
American National Standard for Information Sciences—Permanence of Paper for
Printed Library Materials, ANSI/NISO Z39.48-1992

Dedication

Although Neil Freeman passed to that "undiscovered country" in 2015, his work continues to lead students and actors to a deeper understanding of Shakespeare's plays. With the exception of Shakespeare's words (and my humble foreword), the entirety of the material within these pages is Neil's. May these editions serve as a lasting legacy to a life of dedicated scholarship, and a great passion for Shakespeare.

Contents

FOREWORD

Paul Sugarman

Monologues from Shakespeare's First Folio presents the work of Neil Freeman, longtime champion of Shakespeare's First Folio, whose groundbreaking explorations into how first printings offered insights to the text in rehearsals, stage and in the classroom. This work continued with *Once More Unto the Speech Dear Friends: Monologues from Shakespeare's First Folio with Modern Text Versions for Comparison* where Neil collected over 900 monologues divided between the Comedy, History and Tragedy Published by Applause in three masterful volumes which present the original First Folio text side by side with the modern, edited version of the text. These volumes provide a massive amount of material and information. However both the literary scope, and the literal size of these volumes can be intimidating and overwhelming. This series' intent is to make the work more accessible by taking material from the encyclopediac original volumes and presenting it in an accessible workbook format.

To better focus the work for actors and students the texts are contrasted side by side with introductory notes before and commentary after to aid the exploration of the text. By comparing modern and First Folio printings, Neil points the way to gain new insights into Shakespeare's text. Editors over the centuries have "corrected" and updated the texts to make them "accessible," or "grammatically correct." In doing so they have lost vital clues and information that Shakespeare placed there for his actors. With the texts side by side, you can see where and why editors have made changes and what may have been lost in translation.

In addition to being divided into Histories, Comedies, and Tragedies, the original series further breaks down speeches by the character's designated gender, also indicating speeches appropriate for any gender. Drawing from this example, this series breaks down each original volume into four workbooks: speeches for Women of all ages, Younger Men, Older Men and Any Gender. Gender is naturally fluid for Shakespeare's characters since during his time, ALL of the characters were portrayed by males. Contemporary productions of Shakespeare commonly switch character genders (Prospero has become Prospera), in addition to presenting single gender, reverse gender and gender non-specific productions. There are certainly characters and speeches where the gender is immaterial, hence the inclusion of a volume of speeches for Any Gender. This was something that Neil had indicated in the original volumes; we are merely following his example.

Once More Unto the Speech Dear Friends was a culmination of Neil's dedicated efforts to make the First Folio more accessible and available to readers and to illuminate for actors the many clues within the Folio text, as originally published. The material in this book is drawn from that work and retains Neil's British spelling of words (i.e. capitalisation) and his extensive commentary on each speech. Neil went on to continue this work as a master teacher of Shakespeare with another series of Shakespeare editions, his 'rhythm texts' and the ebook that he published on Apple Books, *The Shakespeare Variations.*

Neil published on his own First Folio editions of the plays in modern type which were the basis the Folio Texts series published by Applause of all 36 plays in the First Folio. These individual editions all have extensive notes on the changes that modern editions had made. This material was then combined to create a complete reproduction of the First Folio in modern type, *The Applause First Folio of Shakespeare in Modern Type.* These editions make the First Folio more accessible than ever before. The examples in this book demonstrate how the clues from the First Folio will give insights to understanding and performing these speeches and why it is a worthwhile endeavour to discover the riches in the First Folio.

PREFACE AND BRIEF BACKGROUND TO THE FIRST FOLIO

WHY ANOTHER SERIES OF SOLILOQUY BOOKS?

There has been an enormous change in theatre organisation recent in the last twenty years. While the major large-scale companies have continued to flourish, many small theatre companies have come into being, leading to

- much doubling
- cross gender casting, with many one time male roles now being played legitimately by/as women in updated time-period productions
- young actors being asked to play leading roles at far earlier points in their careers

All this has meant actors should be able to demonstrate enormous flexibility rather than one limited range/style. In turn, this has meant

- a change in audition expectations
- actors are often expected to show more range than ever before
- often several shorter audition speeches are asked for instead of one or two longer ones
- sometimes the initial auditions are conducted in a shorter amount of time

Thus, to stay at the top of the game, the actor needs more knowledge of what makes the play tick, especially since

- early plays demand a different style from the later ones
- the four genres (comedy, history, tragedy, and the peculiar romances) all have different acting/textual requirements
- parts originally written for the older, more experienced actors again require a different approach from those written for the younger

ones, as the young roles, especially the female ones, were played by young actors extraordinarily skilled in the arts of rhetoric

There's now much more knowledge of how the original quarto and folio texts can add to the rehearsal exploration/acting and directing process as well as to the final performance.

Each speech is made up of four parts

- a background to the speech, placing it in the context of the play, and offering line length and an approximate timing to help you choose what might be right for any auditioning occasion
- a modern text version of the speech, with the sentence structure clearly delineated side by side with
- a folio version of the speech, where modern texts changes to the capitalization, spelling and sentence structure can be plainly seen
- a commentary explaining the differences between the two texts, and in what way the original setting can offer you more information to explore

Thus if they wish, **beginners** can explore just the background and the modern text version of the speech.

An actor experienced in exploring the Folio can make use of the background and the Folio version of the speech

And those wanting to know as many details as possible and how they could help define the deft stepping stones of the arc of the speech can use all four elements on the page.

The First Folio

(FOR LIST OF CURRENT REPRODUCTIONS SEE BIBLIOGRAPHY

The end of 1623 saw the publication of the justifiably famed First Folio (F1). The single volume, published in a run of approximately 1,000 copies at the princely sum of one pound (a tremendous risk, considering that a single play would sell at no more than six pence, one fortieth of F1's price, and that the annual salary of a schoolmaster was only ten pounds), contained thirty-six plays.

The manuscripts from which each F1 play would be printed came from a variety of sources. Some had already been printed. Some came from the playhouse complete with production details. Some had no theatrical input at all, but were handsomely copied out and easy to read. Some were supposedly very messy, complete with first draft scribbles and crossings out. Yet, as Charlton Hinman, the revered dean of First Folio studies describes F1 in the Introduction to the Norton Facsimile:

> It is of inestimable value for what it is, for what it contains. For here are preserved the masterworks of the man universally recognized as our greatest writer; and preserved, as Ben Jonson realized at the time of the original publication, not for an age but for all time.

WHAT DOES F1 REPRESENT?

- texts prepared for actors who rehearsed three days for a new play and one day for one already in the repertoire
- written in a style (rhetoric incorporating debate) so different from ours (grammatical) that many modern alterations based on grammar (or poetry) have done remarkable harm to the rhetorical/debate quality of the original text and thus to interpretations of characters at key moments of stress.
- written for an acting company the core of which steadily grew older, and whose skills and interests changed markedly over twenty years as well as for an audience whose make-up and interests likewise changed as the company grew more experienced

The whole is based upon supposedly the best documents available at the time, collected by men closest to Shakespeare throughout his career, and brought to a single printing house whose errors are now widely understood - far more than those of some of the printing houses that produced the original quartos.

TEXTUAL SOURCES FOR THE AUDITION SPEECHES

Individual modern editions consulted in the preparation of the Modern Text version of the speeches are listed in the Bibliography under the separate headings 'The Complete Works in Compendium Format' and ' The Complete Works in Separate Individual Volumes.' Most of the modern versions of the speeches are a compilation of several of these texts. However, all modern act, scene and/or line numbers refer the reader to The Riverside Shakespeare, in my opinion still the best of the complete works despite the excellent compendiums that have been published since.

The First Folio versions of the speeches are taken from a variety of already published sources, including not only all the texts listed in the 'Photostatted Reproductions in Compendium Format' section of the Bibliography, but also earlier, individually printed volumes, such as the twentieth century editions published under the collective title *The Facsimiles of Plays from The First Folio of Shakespeare* by Faber & Gwyer, and the nineteenth century editions published on behalf of The New Shakespeare Society.

INTRODUCTION

So, congratulations , you've got an audition, and for a Shakespeare play no less.

You've done all your homework, including, hopefully , reading the whole play to see the full range and development of the character.

You've got an idea of the character, the situation in which you/it finds itself (the given circumstance s); what your/its needs are (objectives/ intentions); and what you intend to do about them (action /tactics).

You've looked up all the unusual words in a good dictionary or glossary; you've turned to a well edited modern edition to find out what some of the more obscure references mean.

And those of you who understand metre and rhythm have worked on the poetic values of the speech, and you are word perfect . . .

. . . and yet it's still not working properly and/or you feel there's more to be gleaned from the text , but you're not sure what that something is or how to go about getting at it; in other words, all is not quite right, yet.

THE KEY QUESTION

What text have you been working with - a good modern text or an 'original' text, that is a copy of one of the first printings of the play?

If it's a modern text, no matter how well edited (and there are some splendid single copy editions available, see the Bibliography for further details), despite all the learned information offered, it's not surprising you feel somewhat at a loss, for there is a huge difference between the original printings (the First Folio, and the individual quartos, see

Appendix 1 for further details) and any text prepared after 1700 right up to the most modern of editions. All the post 1700 texts have been tidied-up for the modern reader to ingest silently, revamped according to the rules of correct grammar, syntax and poetry. However the 'originals' were prepared for actors speaking aloud playing characters often in a great deal of emotional and/or intellectual stress, and were set down on paper according to the very flexible rules of rhetoric and a seemingly very cavalier attitude towards the rules of grammar, and syntax, and spelling, and capitalisation, and even poetry.

Unfortunately, because of the grammatical and syntactical standardisation in place by the early 1700's, many of the quirks and oddities of the origin also have been dismissed as 'accidental' - usually as compositor error either in deciphering the original manuscript, falling prey to their own particular idosyncracies, or not having calculated correctly the amount of space needed to set the text. Modern texts dismiss the possibility that these very quirks and oddities may be by Shakespeare, hearing his characters in as much difficulty as poor Peter Quince is in *A Midsummer Night's Dream* (when he, as the Prologue, terrified and struck down by stage fright, makes a huge grammatical hash in introducing his play 'Pyramus and Thisbe' before the aristocracy, whose acceptance or otherwise, can make or break him)

> If we offend, it is with our good will.
> That you should think, we come not to offend,
> But with good will.
> > To show our simple skill,
> That is the true beginning of our end .
> Consider then, we come but in despite.
> We do not come, as minding to content you ,
> Our true intent is.
> > All for your delight
> We are not here.
> > That you should here repent you,

The Actors are at hand; and by their show,
You shall know all, that you are like to know.

(A Midsummer Night's Dream)

In many other cases in the complete works what was originally printed is equally 'peculiar,' but, unlike Peter Quince , these peculiarities are usually regularised by most modern texts.

However, this series of volumes is based on the belief - as the following will show - that most of these 'peculiarities' resulted from Shakespeare setting down for his actors the stresses, trials, and tribulations the characters are experiencing as they think and speak, and thus are theatrical gold-dust for the actor, director, scholar, teacher, and general reader alike.

THE FIRST ESSENTIAL DIFFERENCE BETWEEN THE TWO TEXTS

THINKING

A **modern** text can show

- the story line
- your character's conflict with the world at large
- your character's conflict with certain individuals within that world

but because of the very way an 'original' text was set, it can show you all this plus one key extra, the very thing that makes big speeches what they are

- the conflict within the character

WHY?

Any good playwright writes about characters in stressful situations who are often in a state of conflict not only with the world around them and the people in that world, but also within themselves. And you probably know from personal experience that when these conflicts occur people do not necessarily utter the most perfect of grammatical/poetic/ syntactic statements, phrases, or sentences. Joy and delight, pain and sorrow often come sweeping through in the way things are said, in the incoherence of the phrases, the running together of normally disassociated ideas, and even in the sounds of the words themselves.

The tremendous advantage of the period in which Shakespeare was setting his plays down on paper and how they first appeared in print was that when characters were rational and in control of self and situation, their phrasing and sentences (and poetic structure) would appear to be quite normal even to a modern eye - but when things were going wrong, so sentences and phrasing (and poetic structure) would become highly erratic. But the Quince type eccentricities are rarely allowed to stand. Sadly, in tidying, most modern texts usually make the text far too clean, thus setting rationality when none originally existed.

THE SECOND ESSENTIAL DIFFERENCE BETWEEN THE TWO TEXTS
SPEAKING, ARGUING, DEBATING

Having discovered what and how you/your character is thinking is only the first stage of the work - you/it then have to speak aloud, in a society that absolutely loved to speak - and not only speak ideas (content) but to speak entertainingly so as to keep listeners enthralled (and this was especially so when you have little content to offer and have to mask it somehow - think of today 's television adverts and political spin doctors as a parallel and you get the picture). Indeed one of the Elizabethan 'how to win an argument' books was very precise about this - George Puttenham, *The Art of English Poesie* (1589).

A: ELIZABETHAN SCHOOLING

All educated classes could debate/argue at the drop of a hat, for both boys (in 'petty-schools') and girls (by books and tutors) were trained in what was known overall as the art of rhetoric, which itself was split into three parts

- first, how to distinguish the real from false appearances/outward show (think of the three caskets in *The Merchant of Venice* where the language on the gold and silver caskets enticingly, and deceptively, seems to offer hopes of great personal rewards that are dashed when the language is carefully explored, whereas once the apparent threat on the lead casket is carefully analysed the reward therein is the greatest that could be hoped for)
- second, how to frame your argument on one of 'three great grounds'; honour/morality; justice/legality; and, when all else fails, expedience/practicality.
- third, how to order and phrase your argument so winsomely that your audience will vote for you no matter how good the opposition - and there were well over two hundred rules and variations by which winning could be achieved, all of which had to be assimilated before a child's education was considered over and done with.

B: THINKING ON YOUR FEET: I.E. THE QUICK, DEFT , RAPID MODIFICATION OF EACH TINY THOUGHT

The Elizabethan/therefore your character/therefore you were also trained to explore and modify your thoughts as you spoke - never would you see a sentence in its entirety and have it perfectly worked out in your mind before you spoke (unless it was a deliberately written, formal public declaration, as with the Officer of the Court in The Winter' s Tale, reading the charges against Hermione). Thus after uttering your very first phrase, you might expand it, or modify it, deny it, change it, and so on throughout the whole sentence and speech.

From the poet Samuel Coleridge Taylor there is a wonderful description of how Shakespeare puts thoughts together like "a serpent twisting and untwisting in its own strength," that is, with one thought springing out of the one previous. Treat each new phrase as a fresh unravelling of the serpent's coil. What is discovered (and therefore said) is only revealed as the old coil/phrase disappears revealing a new coil in its place. The new coil is the new thought. The old coil moves/disappears because the previous phrase is finished with as soon as it is spoken.

C: MODERN APPLICATION

It is very rarely we speak dispassionately in our 'real' lives, after all thoughts give rise to feelings, feelings give rise to thoughts, and we usually speak both together - unless

1/ we're trying very hard for some reason to control ourselves and not give ourselves away

2/ or the volcano of emotions within us is so strong that we cannot control ourselves, and feelings swamp thoughts

3/ and sometimes whether deliberately or unconsciously we colour words according to our feelings; the humanity behind the words so revealed is instantly understandable.

D: HOW THE ORIGINAL TEXTS NATURALLY ENHANCE/ UNDERSCORE THIS CONTROL OR RELEASE

The amazing thing about the way all Elizabethan/early Jacobean texts were first set down (the term used to describe the printed words on the page being 'orthography'), is that it was flexible, it allowed for such variations to be automatically set down without fear of grammatical repercussion.

So if Shakespeare heard Juliet's nurse working hard to try to convince Juliet that the Prince's nephew Juliet is being forced to (bigamously) marry, instead of setting the everyday normal

'O he's a lovely gentleman'

which the modern texts HAVE to set, the first printings were permitted to set

'O hee's a Lovely Gentleman'

suggesting that something might be going on inside the Nurse that causes her to release such excessive extra energy.

E: BE CAREFUL

This needs to be stressed very carefully: the orthography doesn't dictate to you/force you to accept exactly what it means. The orthography simply suggests you might want to explore this moment further or more deeply.

In other words, simply because of the flexibility with which the Elizabethans/Shakespeare could set down on paper what they heard in their minds or wanted their listeners to hear, in addition to all the modern acting necessities of character - situation, objective, intention, action, and tactics the original Shakespeare texts offer pointers to where feelings (either emotional or intellectual, or when combined together as passion, both) are also evident.

SUMMARY

BASIC APPROACH TO THE SPEECHES SHOWN BELOW

(after reading the 'background')

1/ first use the modem version shown in the first column: by doing so you can discover

- the basic plot line of what's happening to the character, and
- the first set of conflicts/obstacles impinging on the character as a result of the situation or actions of other characters
- the supposed grammatical and poetical correctnesses of the speech

2/ then you can explore

- any acting techniques you'd apply to any modem soliloquy, including establishing for the character
- the given circumstances of the scene
- their outward state of being (who they are sociologically, etc.)
- their intentions and objectives
- the resultant action and tactics they decide to pursue

3/ when this is complete, turn to the First Folio version of the text, shown on the facing page: this will help you discover and explore

- the precise thinking and debating process so essential to an understanding of any Shakespeare text
- the moments when the text is NOT grammatically or poetically as correct as the modern texts would have you believe, which will in tum help you recognise
- the moments of conflict and struggle stemming from within the character itself
- the sense of fun and enjoyment the Shakespeare language nearly always offers you no matter how dire the situation

4/ should you wish to further explore even more the differences between the two texts, the commentary that follows discusses how the First Folio has been changed, and what those alterations might mean for the human arc of the speech

NOTES ON HOW THESE SPEECHES ARE SET UP

For each of the speeches the first page will include the Background on the speech and other information including number of lines, approximate timing and who is addressed. Then will follow a spread which shows the modern text version on the left and the First Folio version on the right, followed by a page of Commentary.

PROBABLE TIMING: (shown on the Background page before the speeches begin, set below the number of lines) 0.45 = a forty-five second speech

SYMBOLS & ABBREVIATIONS IN THE COMMENTARY AND TEXT

F: the First Folio

mt.: modern texts

F # followed by a number: the number of the sentence under discussion in the First Folio version of the speech, thus F #7 would refer to the seventh sentence

mt. # followed by a numb er: the number of the sentence under discussion in the modern text version of the speech, thus mt. #5 would refer to the fifth sentence

 # /#, (e.g. 3/7): the first number refers to the number of capital letters in the passage under discussion; the second refers to the number of long spellings therein

within a quotation from the speech: / indicates where one verse line ends and a fresh one starts

[ ] : set around words in both texts when F1 sets one word , mt another

{ } : some minor alteration has been made, in a speech built up, where, a word or phrase will be changed, added, or removed

{†} : this symbol shows where a sizeable part of the text is omitted

TERMS FOUND IN THE COMMENTARY
OVERALL

1/ **orthography**: the capitalization, spellings, punctuation of the First Folio
SIGNS OF IMPORTANT DISCOVERIES/ARGUMENTS WITHIN
A FIRST FOLIO SPEECH

2/ **major punctuation**: colons and semicolons: since the Shakespeare texts
are based so much on the art of debate and argument, the importance of
F1 's major punctuation must not be underestimated, for both the semicolon (;) and colon (:) mark a moment of importance for the character,
either for itself, as a moment of discovery or revelation, or as a key point
in a discussion, argument or debate that it wishes to impress upon other
characters onstage

as a rule of thumb:

a/ the more frequent colon (:) suggests that whatever the power of the
point discovered or argued, the character is not side-tracked and can continue with the argument - as such, the colon can be regarded as a **logical**
connection

b/ the far less frequent semicolon (;) suggests that because of the power
inherent in the point discovered or argued, the character is side-tracked
and momentarily loses the argument and falls back into itself or can only
continue the argument with great difficulty - as such, the semicolon should
be regarded as an **emotional** connection

3/ **surround phrases**: phrase(s) surrounded by major punctuation, or a
combination of major punctuation and the end or beginning of a sentence:
thus these phrases seem to be of especial importance for both character
and speech, well worth exploring as key to the argument made and /or
emotions released

DIALOGUE NOT FOUND IN THE FIRST FOLIO
∞ set where modern texts add dialogue from a quarto text which has
not been included in Fl

A LOOSE RULE OF THUMB TO THE THINKING PROCESS OF A FIRST FOLIO CHARACTER

1/ mental discipline/**intellect**: a section where capitals dominate suggests that the intellectual reason ing behind what is being spoken or discovered is of more concern than the personal response beneath it

2/ feelings/**emotions**: a section where long spellings dominate suggests that the personal response to what is being spoken or discovered is of more concern than the intellectual reasoning behind it

3/ **passion**: a section where both long spellings and capitals are present in almost equal proportions suggests that both mind and emotion/feelings are inseparable, and thus the character is speaking passionately

SIGNS OF LESS THAN GRAMMATICAL THINKING WITHIN A FIRST FOLIO SPEECH

1/ **onrush**: sometimes thoughts are coming so fast that several topics are joined together as one long sentence suggesting that the F character's mind is working very quickly, or that his/her emotional state is causing some concern: most mod ern texts split such a sentence into several grammatically correct parts (the opening speech of *As You Like It* is a fine example, where F's long 18 line opening sentence is split into six): while the modern texts' resetting may be syntactically correct, the F moment is nowhere near as calm as the revisions suggest

2/ **fast-link**: sometimes F shows thoughts moving so quickly for a character that the connecting punctuation between disparate topics is merely a comma, suggesting that there is virtually no pause in springing from one idea to the next: unfortunately most modern texts rarely allow this to stand, instead replacing the obviously disturbed comma with a grammatical period, once more creating calm that it seems the original texts never intended to show

FIRST FOLIO SIGNS OF WHEN VERBAL GAME PLAYING HAS TO STOP

1/ **non-embellished:** a section with neither capitals nor long spellings suggests that what is being discovered or spoken is so important to the character that there is no time to guss it up with vocal or mental excesses: an unusual moment of self-control

2/ **short sentence:** coming out of a society where debate was second nature, man y of Shakespeare's characters speak in long sentences in which ideas are stated, explored, redefined and summarized all before moving onto the next idea in the argument, discovery or debate: the longer sentence is the sign of a rhetorically trained mind used to public speaking (oratory), but at times an idea or discovery is so startling or inevitable that length is either unnecessary or impossible to maintain : hence the occasional very important short sentence suggests that there is no time for the niceties of oratorical adornment with which to sugar the pill - verbal games are at an end and now the basic core of the issue must be faced

3/ **monosyllabic:** with English being composed of two strands, the polysyllabic (stemming from French, Italian, Latin and Greek), and the monosyllabic (from the Anglo-Saxon), each strand has two distinct functions: the polysyllabic words are often used when there is time for fanciful elaboration and rich description (which could be described as 'excessive rhetoric') while the monosyllabic occur when, literally, there is no other way of putting a basic question or comment - Juliet's "Do you love me? I know thou wilt say aye" is a classic example of both monosyllables and non-embellishment: with monosyllables, only the naked truth is being spoken, nothing is hidden

Monologues from Shakespeare's First Folio for Younger Men: *The Comedies*

The Comedie of Errors
Antipholus V.

Sweete Mistris, what your name is else I know not;
3.2.29–52

Background: the visting Antipholus's immediate, and obviously high-ly smitten, response to Luciana's passionate advice. (As part of the chivalric code/approach to courtly love young men were expected, indeed encouraged, to fall in love at first sight—see Protheus in *Two Gentlemen of Verona*; all four young men in *Love's Labours Lost*; and Romeo).

Style: speech as part of a two-handed scene

Where: somewhere private in Adriana's home

To Whom: Luciana

# of Lines: 24

Probable Timing: 1.15 minutes

Take Note: The onrush of F's final sentence (#5) is one indication of how much Antipholus' passions have been roused by Luciana's mis-taken identity advice. And if this weren't enough, the many sur-round phrases underscore the fervency of his feelings (the releases an emotional 3/29 overall). Most modern texts create a much more rational finish by splitting F#5 into three grammatically correct units.

Antipholus V.

1   Sweet mistress—what your name is else I know not,
     Nor by what wonder you do hit of mine—
     Less in your knowledge and your grace you show not
     [Than] our earth's wonder, more [than] earth divine .

2   Teach me, dear creature, how to think and speak :
     Lay open to my earthy, gross conceit,
     Smoth'red in errors, feeble, shallow, weak,
     The folded meaning of your word's deceit .

3   Against my soul's pure truth, why labor you,
     To make it wander in an unknown field ?

4   Are you a god ?

5   Would you create me new ?

6   Transform me then, and to your pow'r I'll yield.

7   But if that I am I, then well I know
     Your weeping sister is no wife of mine,
     Nor to her bed no homage do I owe :
     Far more, far more, to you do I decline .

8   O, train me not, sweet mermaid, with thy note,
     To drown me in thy [sister's] flood of tears.

9   Sing, siren, for thyself, and I will dote ;
     Spread o'er the silver waves thy golden hairs,
     And as a [bed] I'll take [them], and there lie,
     And in that glorious supposition think
     He gains by death that hath such means to die :
     Let love, being light, be drowned if she sink !

Antipholus V.

1   Sweete Mistris, what your name is else I know not;
Nor by what wonder you do hit of mine :
Lesse in your knowledge, and your grace you show not,
[Then] our earths wonder, more[then] earth divine .

2   Teach me deere creature how to thinke and speake :
Lay open to my earthie grosse conceit :
Smothred in errors, feeble, shallow, weake,
The foulded meaning of your words deceit :
Against my soules pure truth, why labour you,
To make it wander in an unknowne field ?

3   Are you a god ? would you create me new ?

4   Transforme me then, and to your powre Ile yeeld .

5   But if that I am I, then well I know,
Your weeping sister is no wife of mine,
Nor to her bed no homage doe I owe :
Farre more, farre more, to you doe I decline :
Oh traine me not sweet Mermaide, with thy note,
To drowne me in thy [sister] floud of teares :
Sing Siren for thy selfe, and I will dote :
Spread ore the silver waves thy golden haires;
And as a [bud] Ile take [thee], and there lie :
And in that glorious supposition thinke,
He gaines by death, that hath such meanes to die :
Let Love, being light, be drowned if she sinke .

- the first two sentences start very strongly, with F #1 (a declaration of wonder) opening with two surround phrases, heightened by being linked with an emotional semicolon

   " . Sweete Mistris, what your name is else I know not ; /Nor by what wonder you do hit of mine : "

   and F #2 ('Teach me') also starting with two surround phrases,

   " . Teach me deere creature how to thinke and speake : /Lay open to my earthie grosse conceit :"

- and the 'love-struckness' continues with two one line sentences, the first (F#3's 'Are you a god?') heightened by being breath-takingly un-embellished, and the second (F #4's 'Transforme me') being much more emotional (0/2 in one line)

- within the onrushed last sentence surround phrases again point to his total abandoning of himself to her

" : Farre more, farre more, to you doe I decline : /…: /Sing Siren for thy selfe, and I will dote : /Spread ore the silver waves thy golden haires ; /And as a [bud] Ile take [thee], and there lie : "

- some of the clustered releases point to moments where his passion breaks through even more, as 'Teach me deere creature how to thinke and speake:'; 'Transforme me then, and to your powre Ile yeeld.'; and then the three line extravaganza 'Farre more, farre more, to you doe I decline :

   /Oh traine me not sweet Mermaide, with thy note, /To drowne me in thy [sister] floud of teares :'

- yet at times the unembellished lines speak to his sense of wonder 'Are you a god? would you create me new?'; his desire for Luciana to understand he is free to woo her legitimately 'But if that I am I, then well I know/Your weeping sister is no wife of mine,'; and his desire to be with her, asking her to spread her hair so that 'And as a bud Ile take thee and there lie:'

The Two Gentlemen of Verona
Valentine

I Protheus, but that life is alter'd now,
2.4.128–142

Background: Valentine, a young man of Verona, has embarked on the 'grand tour', as all young men of his generation should; in his case to Milan. Originally, his friend Protheus, in love with Julia, did not join him, and Valentine roundly mocked Protheus for being in love. At his father's insistence, Protheus has joined Valentine in Milan, where Valentine is now singing a completely different tune, for he is now totally (and mutually) in love, with Silvia, the Duke of Milan's daughter.

Style: speech as part of a two handed conversation

Where: somewhere in the Duke of Milan's palace

To Whom: his friend Protheus

# of Lines: 15

Probable Timing: 0.50 minutes

Take note: Rather than the controlled, almost reflective, short sentence opening of most modern texts, F suggests, via the onrushed fast-link comma at the end of F #1's first line, that the love-struck Valentine is quite disturbed by his new found love experiences, both the painful and the occasional nourishing delight.

Valentine

1   Ay, Protheus, but that life is alter'd now .

2   I have done penance for contemning Love,
     Whose high imperious thoughts have punish'd me
     With bitter fasts, with penitential groans,
     With nightly tears, and daily heart-sore sighs,
     For in revenge of my contempt of love,
     Love hath chas'd sleep from my enthralled eyes,
     And made them watchers of mine own heart's sorrow .

3   O gentle Protheus, Love's a mighty lord,
     And hath so humbled me, as I confess
     There is no woe to his correction,
     Nor to his service, no such joy on earth :
     Now no discourse, except it be of love ;
     Now can I break my fast, dine, sup, and sleep,
     Upon the very naked name of love .

Valentine

1   I Protheus, but that life is alter'd now,
     I have done pennance for contemning Love,
     Whose high emperious thoughts have punish'd me
     With bitter fasts, with penitentiall grones,
     With nightly teares, and daily hart-sore sighes,
     For in revenge of my contempt of love,
     Love hath chas'd sleepe from my enthralled eyes,
     And made them watchers of mine owne hearts sorrow .

2   O gentle Protheus, Love's a mighty Lord,
     And hath so humbled me, as I confesse
     There is no woe to his correction,
     Nor to his Service, no such joy on earth :
     Now, no discourse, except it be of love :
     Now can I breake my fast, dine, sup, and sleepe,
     Upon the very naked name of Love .

- the non-embellished phrases clearly show how and why

    "For in revenge of my contempt of love,"

    "There is no woe to his correction,"

    while the last is doubly weighted by being the only surround line in the speech

    " : Now, no discourse, except it be of love : "

- not surprisingly, Valentine's F#1 confession of 'fasts', 'grones', 'teares' and 'sighes' is highly emotional (2/6)

- however, the definition of humbling 'Love' as a 'mighty Lord' is strongly intellectual (4/1 in the first four lines of F #2, to the first colon)

- though the final summary as to how he can now eat and sleep 'Upon the very naked name of Love' becomes somewhat emotional once more (1/2, the last two lines of F #2)

The Two Gentlemen of Verona
Protheus

I will ./Even as one heate, another heate expels,
2.4.191–214

Background: Protheus has just met the Duke of Milan's daughter Silvia, and, despite Valentine's confession of his and Silvia's mutual love (prior speech) and though, before leaving Verona, Protheus and Julia became betrothed, Protheus has fallen head over heels for Silvia too!

Style: solo

Where: somewhere in the Duke of Milan's palace

To Whom: direct audience address

# of Lines: 23

Probable Timing: 1.10 minutes

Take Note: While the speech is somewhat emotional overall (6/14), the fact that there are only fourteen emotional releases in twenty-four lines, together with the presence of at least eight non-embellished lines, suggests that Protheus is working very hard to stay calm, trying to make sense of what has just occurred. However, F's opening sentence structure (much altered by most modern texts) shows that, at times, rationality is difficult to come by.

Protheus

1   I will .

2   Even as one heat another heat expels,
     Or as one nail by strength drives out another ,
     So the remembrance of my former love
     Is by a newer object quite forgotten .

4   [Is it] mine [eye], or Valentines praise ,
     Her true perfection, or my false transgression ,
     That makes me reasonless, to reason thus ?

5   She is faire, and so is Julia that I love
     (That I did love, for now my love is thaw'd,
     Which like a waxen image 'gainst a fire
     Bears no impression of the thing it was .)

6   [Methinks] my zeal to Valentine is cold,
     And that I love him not as I was wont :
     O, but I love his lady too-too much,
     And that's the reason I love him so little .

7   How shall I dote on her with more advice,
     That thus without advice begin to love her ?

8   'Tis but her picture I have yet beheld,
     And that hath dazzled my [reason's] light ;
     But when I look on her perfections,
     There is no reason but I shall be blind .

9   If I can check my erring love, I will;
     If not, to compass her I'll use my skill .

Protheus

1   I will .

2   Even as one heate, another heate expels,
    Or as one naile, by strength drives out another .

3   So the remembrance of my former Love
    Is by a newer object quite forgotten,
    [It is] mine [ ], or Valentines praise ?
    Her true perfection, or my false transgression ?
    That makes me reasonlesse, to reason thus ?

4   Shee is faire :and so is Julia that I love,
    (That I did love, for now my love is thaw'd,
    Which like a waxen Image 'gainst a fire
    Beares no impression of the thing it was .)

5   [Me thinkes] my zeale to Valentine is cold,
    And that I love him not as I was wont :
    O, but I love his Lady too-too much,
    And that's the reason I love him so little .

6   How shall I doate on her with more advice,
    That thus without advice begin to love her ?

7   'Tis but her picture I have yet beheld,
    And that hath dazel'd my [reasons] light :
    But when I looke on her perfections,
    There is no reason, but I shall be blinde .

8   If I can checke my erring love, I will,
    If not, to compasse her Ile use my skill .

- the ungrammatical period establishing F #2 as a separate sentence underscores the enormity of Protheus' realisation that Silvia has driven all thoughts of Julia out of his mind: most modern texts follow the Second Folio and set the 'correct' punctuation (colon or comma), thus removing the emotional need to pause and regroup before continuing: similarly F's again ungrammatical setting (in the eyes of most modern texts) of a fast-link comma at the end of F #3's line two shows just how much Protheus' thoughts are now racing ahead unchecked: once more, most modern texts set the logically correct punctuation (here a period), thus holding him to a much more rational process than originally set

- the one highly emotional surround phrase ' Shee is faire : ' points to the impact the brief meeting with Silvia has had upon him

- it's the calm of the unembellished lines that show how seriously Protheus is trying to come to terms with all the implications of his new 'at-first-sight' love

    'Even as one heate…/by strength drives out another .', so Julia 'Is by a newer object quite forgotten,…/[Is it] mine…/Her true perfection, or my false transgression ?/That makes me…, to reason thus ?'

then comes the realisation about both Julia 'That I did love, for now my love is thaw'd,' and his former friend Valentine 'And that I love him not as I was wont', because now they both will be rivals for Silvia 'And that's the reason I love him so little .' finishing with the understanding he is both alone and foolishly in love (having met Silvia for about thirty seconds) 'That thus without advice begin to love her ? /'Tis but her picture I have yet beheld,/And that hath dazel'd my reasons light :'

The Taming of the Shrew

Lucentio

Tranio, since for the great desire I had
1.1.1–24

Background: his first speech in the play sets up exactly who and what he is.

Style: as part of a two-handed scene

Where: unspecified, but presumably a public place/street in Padua

To Whom: his man-servant Tranio

# of Lines: 24

Probable Timing: 1.15 minutes

Take Note: This opening speech is often played as one of great braggadocio, as might befit the audience grabbing first lines of the play within the play. Yet, the mix of non-embellished lines, three extra breath-thoughts at key times, virtual lack of logical punctuation (just two colons), and overall intellectual weight over emotion (18/10), all support the idea of Lucentio being a young man on his first trip away from home, and none too sure of himself.

Lucentio

1   Tranio, since for the great desire I had
    To see fair Padua, nursery of arts,
    I am arriv'd for fruitful Lombardy,
    The pleasant garden of great Italy,
    And by my father's love and leave am arm'd
    With his good will and thy good company,
    My trusty servant, well approv'd in all,
    Here let us breath, and haply institute
    A course of learning and ingenious studies .

2   Pisa, renowned for grave citizens,
    Gave me my being and my father first
    A merchant of great traffic through the world,
    [Vincentio,] come of the Bentivolii;
    Vincentio's son, brought up in Florence,
    It shall become to serve all hopes conceiv'd,
    To deck his fortune with his virtuous deeds .

3   And therefore, Tranio, for the time I study,
    Virtue and that part of philosophy
    Will I apply, that treats of happiness
    By virtue specially to be achiev'd .

4   Tell me thy mind, for I have Pisa left
    And am to Padua come, as he that leaves
    A shallow plash, to plunge him in the deep,
    And with satiety seeks to quench his thirst .

Lucentio

1　Tranio, since for the great desire I had
　　To see faire Padua, nurserie of Arts,
　　I am arriv'd for fruitfull Lumbardie,
　　The pleasant garden of great Italy,
　　And by my fathers love and leave am arm'd
　　With his good will, and thy good companie .

2　My trustie servant well approv'd in all,
　　Heere let us breath, and haply institute
　　A course of Learning, and ingenious studies .

3　Pisa renowned for grave Citizens
　　Gave me my being, and my father first
　　A Merchant of great Trafficke through the world :
　　[Vincentio's] come of the Bentivoly,
　　Vincentio's sonne, brought up in Florence,
　　It shall become to serve all hopes conceiv'd
　　To decke his fortune with his vertuous deedes :
　　And therefore Tranio, for the time I studie,
　　Vertue and that part of Philosophie
　　Will I applie, that treats of happinesse,
　　By vertue specially to be atchiev'd .

4　Tell me thy minde, for I have Pisa left,
　　And am to Padua come, as he that leaves
　　A shallow plash, to plunge him in the deepe,
　　And with sacietie seekes to quench his thirst .

- the unembellished lines point to his youth and need for guidance from others

  "And by my fathers love and leave am arm'd/With his good will and thy good companie ." along with "My trustie servant well approv'd in all,"

  plus his initial determination to be a good student to study 'Vertue' and 'Philosophie', so as to get the rewards 'By vertue specially to be atchiev'd'

- dealing with their arrival in Padua, the speech opens intellectually (5/2 in F #1's first four lines), followed by a non-embellished reference to his father to finish the sentence (scared of him perhaps?—which would certainly explain his and Tranio's behaviour towards the real Vincentio later in the play)

- F #2 approaches the subject of learning quite gingerly (1/1 in three lines)

- the praise of his own family and city background is highly (proudly?) intellectual (8/2 in the first five lines of F #3), while the next two lines, hoping to be a credit to his father, become monetarily emotional (0/2)

- in F #3's final four lines, the hopes for the rewards of study move from intellect (2/0 to the first two lines), through emotion (the penultimate line), to neutrality (the last line)—perhaps he is not a particularly good student (certainly he is not particularly smart in the ways of the world as later actions in the play clearly show)

- but it seems he manages to recover his spirits, for the final sentence, where he essentially puts himself in Tranio's hands, becomes passionate (2/3, F #4)

The Taming of the Shrew

Lucentio

Oh Tranio, till I found it to be true,
1.1.148–158 (with inserts from 1.1.167–170 & 1.1.174–176)

Background: Lucentio, as many young men in the Shakespeare comedies, has fallen in love at first sight, unfortunately with Bianca, who,
as seen above, is being fought over by the two local wooers. As to
the classical references,
1. Agenor's daughter was Europa, whose beauty so moved Jupiter
(Jove) that he changed himself into a bull on whose back she
crossed the sea to Crete whereupon he resumed his true shape
and successfully wooed her
2. the Queen of Carthage was Dido, Anna her sister and confidant

Style: as part of a two-handed scene

Where: unspecified, but presumably a public place/street in Padua

To Whom: Tranio

# of Lines: 18

Probable Timing: 0.55 minutes

Take Note: Bianca's impact on Lucentio is beautifully underscored by
the slow start building to an enormous release by the finish.

Lucentio

1   O Tranio, till I found it to be true,
       I never thought it possible or likely .

2   But see, while idly I stood looking on,
       I found the effect of love in idleness,

{insert 1}   {I saw sweet beauty in her face,
       Such as the daughter of Agenor had,
       That made great Jove to humble him to her hand,
       When with his knees he kiss'd the Cretan strand .}

{insert 2} 3   {Tranio, I saw her coral lips to move,
       And with her breath she did perfume the air.

4   Sacred and sweet was all I saw in her }{,}
       And now in plainness do confess to thee,
       That art to me as secret and as dear
       As Anna to the Queen of Carthage was :
       Tranio, I burn, I pine, I perish, Tranio,
       If I achieve not this young modest girl .

5   Counsel me, Tranio, for I know thou canst :
       Assist me, Tranio, for I know thou wilt .

Lucentio

1   Oh Tranio, till I found it to be true,
     I never thought it possible or likely .

2   But see, while idely I stood looking on,
     I found the effect of Love in idlenesse,

{insert 1}   {I saw sweet beautie in her face,
     Such as the daughter of Agenor had,
     That made great Jove to humble him to her hand,
     When with his knees he kist the Cretan strond .}

{insert 2} 3   {Tranio, I saw her corrall lips to move,
     And with her breath she did perfume the ayre,
     Sacred and sweet was all I saw in her }{,}
     And now in plainnesse do confesse to thee
     That art to me as secret and as deere
     As Anna to the Queene of Carthage was :
     Tranio I burne, I pine, I perish Tranio,
     If I atchieve not this yong modest gyrle :
     Counsaile me Tranio, for I know thou canst :
     Assist me Tranio, for I know thou wilt .

- what struck him most is spoken quietly without any embellishment, '…till I found it to be true,/I never thought it possible or likely ./But see, while idely I stood looking on,' which leads to 'Sacred and sweet was all I saw in her"

- while his need for Tranio's help is highlighted by the only two surround phrases of the speech that end the speech, ' : Counsaile me Tranio, for I know thou canst : / Assist me Tranio, for I know thou wilt .'—the plea made even stronger by a faster release without the extra modern commas (shown in the F text by the)

- after Lucentio's somewhat 'gob-smacked' first two words ('Oh Tranio'), the rest of F #1 is breath-takingly quiet, while F #2 becomes carefully factual in the classical references to her (4/1 in the six lines), as if trying not disturb the vision perhaps?

- but, once he describes her physical attributes, so passion bursts through (0/5 in F #3's first five lines), while his fervent last five lines expressing 'I burne, I pine, I perish' becomes intellectually passionate (8/4)

The Taming of the Shrew
Petruchio

But will {I} woo this Wilde-cat ?
1.2.197–210

Background: Hortentio has introduced Petruchio to Bianca-wooing-rival Gremio, whose doubt that Petruchio will woo 'this Wilde-cat' gives rise to the following.

Style: address primarily to two people as part of a four handed scene

Where: outside Hortentio's home

To Whom: initially to the would-be-Bianca-wooer Gremio, and then expands the speech to include both his friend Hortentio and his own servant, Grumio

# of Lines: 15

Probable Timing: 0.50 minutes

Take Note: With the speech displaying no colons, and the fact that five of the nine sentences are short, it would seem that rather, than a statement of already absorbed philosophy, Petruchio is discovering/improvising as he goes.

Petruchio

1 But will {I} woo this wildcat ?

---

2 Why came I hither but to that intent ?

3 Think you, a little din can daunt mine ears ?

4 Have I not in my time heard lions roar ?

5 Have I not heard the sea, puff'd up with winds,
  Rage like an angry boar chafed with sweat ?

6 Have I not heard great ordnance in the field,
  And heavens artillery thunder in the skies ?

7 Have I not in a pitched battle heard
  Loud 'larums, neighing steeds, & trumpets' clang ?

8 And do you tell me of a woman's tongue,
  That gives not half so great a blow to hear
  As will a chestnut in a farmer's fire .

9 Tush, tush, fear boys with bugs {,} for {I fear} none .

Petruchio

1 But will {I} woo this Wilde-cat ?

---

2 Why came I hither, but to that intent ?

3 Thinke you, a little dinne can daunt mine eares ?

4 Have I not in my time heard Lions rore ?

5 Have I not heard the sea, puft up with windes,
   Rage like an angry Boare, chafed with sweat ?

6 Have I not heard great Ordnance in the field ?
   And heavens Artillerie thunder in the skies ?

7 Have I not in a pitched battell heard
   Loud larums, neighing steeds, & trumpets clangue ?

8 And do you tell me of a womans tongue ?
   That gives not halfe so great a blow to heare,
   As wil a Chesse-nut in a Farmers fire .

9 Tush, tush, feare boyes with bugs {,} {*}
   For {I feare} none .

- orthographically, the speech falls into two halves; a slow building intellectual and emotional start (5/4 in the first eight lines, F #1-6), and then a highly emotional finale (2/8 in the last six and a half lines, F #7-9)

- given the slow build of the opening, the sudden intense emotional release of F #3's 'Thinke you, a little dinne can daunt mine eares?' seems splendidly braggadocio, while it may be Petruchio is trying to persuade himself as well as others of his bravery with the intellectual concentration of F #6's 'Have I not heard great Ordnance in the field ? /And heavens Artillerie thunder in the skies?', especially with the F only question-mark at the end of the first line, since the Elizabethan question mark also functions as an exclamation point

- similarly, the final release of F #8's 'Tush, tush, feare boyes with bugs,/ For I feare none.' has a splendid flourishing ring to it

- also, it could be that Petruchio is attempting to calm himself down, or convince others of his calm, with the two unembellished lines: F #2's 'Why came I hither, but to that intent?' (especially with the extra breath-thought, marked ,) and F #8's opening line 'And do you tell me of a womans tongue?', again with the F only question mark/ exclamation point

The Taming of the Shrew

Petruchio

Now by the world, it is a lustie Wench,
between 2.1.160–181

Background: all the wooers have now been introduced to and accepted by Baptista, two as themselves viz. Petruchio to woo Kate, and Gremio to woo Bianca, and three in various disguises, all intending to woo Bianca, viz. Tranio disguised as Lucentio; Lucentio disguised as Cambio a schoolteacher; and Hortentio, who has decided to go under-cover as a music teacher (calling himself Litio) so as to have private access to Bianca (just as the real Lucentio has done). The disguised Hortentio has just come back from attempting to teach music to Kate, who hit him so forcibly with the lute that 'through the instrument my pate made way'. All eyes are now on Petruchio to see how he will react and what he will do.

Style: the first three lines to a large group, the remainder as a solo

Where: at Baptista's home

To Whom: initially Baptista, Gremio, the injured Hortentio, and Tranio pretending to be Lucentio, then self and direct audience address

# of Lines: 16

Probable Timing: 0.50 minutes

Take Note: With their first five sentences, most modern texts offer a far more rational Petruchio than F's original two onrushed sentences show. That in F he displays nowhere near as much self-control can be seen in the overall pattern of releases in the speech (4/12).

Petruchio

1   Now by the world, it is a lusty wench!

2   I love her ten times more [than] e'er I did .

3   O, how I long to have some chat with her .

---

4   {I'll} woo her with some spirit when she comes .

5   Say that she rail, why then I'll tell her plain
     She sings as sweetly as a nightingale ;
     Say that she frown, I'll say she looks as clear
     As morning roses newly wash'd with dew ;
     Say she be mute, and will not speak a word,
     Then I'll commend her volubility,
     And say she uttereth piercing eloquence ;
     If she do bid me pack, I'll give her thanks,
     As though she bid me stay by her a week ;
     If she deny to wed, I'll crave the day
     When I shall ask the banes, and when be married .

6   But here she comes, and now, Petruchio, speak .

Petruchio

1   Now by the world, it is a lustie Wench,
I love her ten times more [then] ere I did,
Oh how I long to have some chat with her .

---

2   {Ile} woo her with some spirit when she comes,
Say that she raile, why then Ile tell her plaine,
She sings as sweetly as a Nightinghale :
Say that she frowne, Ile say she lookes as cleere
As morning Roses newly washt with dew :
Say she be mute, and will not speake a word,
Then Ile commend her volubility,
And say she uttereth piercing eloquence :
If she do bid me packe, Ile give her thankes,
As though she bid me stay by her a weeke :
If she denie to wed, Ile crave the day
When I shall aske the banes, and when be married .

3   But heere she comes, and now Petruchio speake .

- in the onrushed F #1, although the images in the monosyllabic non-embellished line 'I love her ten times more than ere I did' followed by the equally monosyllabic phrase 'how I long to have some chat with her' seem splendidly brave, the style hardly matches the substance—raising the questions just who this is for? and how brave is he really feeling?

- within the onrushed F #2, the non-embellished lines show that Petruchio's wasting no energy as he discovers a possible plan,

  "Ile woo her with some spirit when she comes,"

  realising opposites may work, for example

  "Say she be mute … / Then Ile commend her volubility, /And say she uttereth piercing eloquence" and

  "If she denie to wed, Ile crave the day … and when be married."

  the discoveries perhaps forcing him to a state of apparent calmness

- the release in the final one line sentence (1/2, F #3) speaks volumes as to his whole state, especially given his inability to continue his previous onrush (through apprehension perhaps)

The Taming of the Shrew

Petruchio

O Kate content thee, prethee be not angry .
between 3.2.215–235

Background: having destroyed two highly bourgeois conventional traits of any mercantile wedding through his impossible attire and behaviour, Petruchio now uses a mercantile analysis to describe Kate as his possession, which in many ways parallels the way Bianca was auctioned off to the highest bidder. Whether this is genuine boorish behaviour or a deliberate attempt in part to show Kate just how appalling the society she is already at odds with is and in part to keep everyone off balance is up to each production to decide. What triggers the speech is Kate's public insistence that, though Petruchio has stated they must leave straight away and not wait for the wedding feast, she has commanded that the Gentlemen go 'forward to the bridall dinner', telling her father for all to hear that Petruchio 'shall stay my leisure'.

Style: public address to the assembled company at large

Where: as above

To Whom: initially Kate and then to Baptista, Bianca, the disguised Tranio, Gremio, Grumio, Biondello, perhaps Lucentio and Hortentio, plus however many guests the acting company can afford

# of Lines: 15

Probable Timing: 0.50 minutes

Petruchio

1   O Kate, content thee, prithee be not angry .

---

2   They shall go forward, Kate, at thy command .

3   Obey the bride, you that attend on her .

4   Go to the feast, revel and domineer,
     Carouse full measure to her maiden head,
     Be mad and merry, or go hang your selves ;
     But for my bonny Kate, she must with me .

5   Nay, look not big, nor stamp, nor stare, nor fret,
     I will be master of what is mine own.

6   She is my goods, my chattels, she is my house,
     My household stuff, my field, my barn,
     My horse, my ox, my ass, my any thing :
     And here she stands, touch her who ever dare,
     I'll bring mine action on the proudest he
     That stops my way in Padua .

Petruchio

1   O Kate content thee, prethee be not angry .

---

2   They shall goe forward Kate at thy command,
    Obey the Bride you that attend on her .

3   Goe to the feast, revell and domineere,
    Carowse full measure to her maiden-head,
    Be madde and merry, or goe hang your selves :
    But for my bonny Kate, she must with me :
    Nay, looke not big, nor stampe, nor stare, nor fret,
    I will be master of what is mine owne,
    Shee is my goods, my chattels, she is my house,
    My houshold-stuffe, my field, my barne,
    My horse, my oxe, my asse, my any thing,
    And heere she stands, touch her who ever dare,
    Ile bring mine action on the proudest he
    That stops my way in Padua :

Take Note: F's sentence structure suggests a deceptively calm and rational opening (F #1-2 matched with mt.'s #1-2), which is then blown apart by one long final F #3 onrush, the impact of which most modern texts reduce by splitting F #3 into three.

- the deceptively calm opening is matched by an apparent intellectual calm (3/1), coupled with two small unembellished phrases addressed to Kate that also seem to suggest a (as it turns out unwarranted) calm: 'content thee, prethee be not angry.'

- and once the onrush comes, it comes with an enormously full emotional release (2/15 in the twelve lines of F #3)

- it is fascinating that the long-spelled words do not come in clusters in this case, but rather seem to fall as one per phrase, as if his argument were emotionally important to him—perhaps an attack on the very bourgeois beliefs of all present that allowed Kate's sister Bianca to be auctioned off to the highest bidder

- thus the one double release ('revell and domineere,') coming as it does at the start of F #3, may be deceptive, serving only to grab the listeners' attention to 'yet another Petruchio harangue' before moving into something rather more serious

- the colon ending the speech suggests that Petruchio hasn't really finished, but rather is still energised awaiting and any challenge that may come his way as a result of what he has just said

The Taming of the Shrew

Petruchio

Thus have I politickely begun my reigne,
4.1.118–211

Background: having reached home in Verona, Petruchio's startling ways continue. Faced with a rabble of incompetent servants, he has destroyed the meal provided for himself and Kate, thus ensuring she goes to bed without any nourishment—which is all part of his plan, as he now explains.

Style: solo

Where: unspecified, somewhere in Petruchio's home

To Whom: direct audience address, ending with a challenge

# of Lines: 24

Probable Timing: 1.15 minutes

Take Note: F's onrushed three sentences suggest a man discovering what might work, not a character explaining what he already knows is going to be successful. Not only do most modern texts reset the speech as seven sentences, thus rendering Petruchio far more rational than F suggests, they also transfer the triumphant, sentence-ending 'She eate no meate to day, nor none shall eate.' (end of F #2) to start a new idea (mt. #4), reducing the 'I've done it' of the original to a mere first stepping stone in a further litany of deprivations.

Petruchio

1   Thus have I politicly begun my reign,
    And 'tis my hope to end successfully .

2   My falcon now is sharp and passing empty,
    And till she stoop, she must not be full-gorg'd,
    For then she never looks upon her lure .

3   Another way I have to man my haggard,
    To make her come, and know her keeper's call,
    That is, to watch her, as we watch these kites
    That bait, and beat, and will not be obedient .

4   She eat no meat to day, nor none shall eat;
    Last night she slept not, nor to night she shall not ;
    As with the meat, some undeserved fault
    I'll find about the making of the bed,
    And here I'll fling the pillow, there the bolster,
    This way the coverlet, another way the sheets .

5   Ay, and amid this hurly I intend
    That all is done in reverend care of her,
    And in conclusion, she shall watch all night,
    And if she chance to nod I'll rail and brawl,
    And with the clamor keep her still awake .

6   This is a way to kill a wife with kindness,
    And thus I'll curb her mad and headstrong humor .

7   He that knows better how to tame a shrew,
    Now let him speak; 'tis charity to shew .

Petruchio

1   Thus have I politickely begun my reigne,
And 'tis my hope to end successefully :
My Faulcon now is sharpe, and passing emptie,
And til she stoope, she must not be full gorg'd,
For then she never lookes upon her lure .

2   Another way I have to man my Haggard,
To make her come, and know her Keepers call :
That is, to watch her, as we watch these Kites,
That baite, and beate, and will not be obedient :
She eate no meate to day, nor none shall eate .

3   Last night she slept not, nor to night she shall not :
As with the meate, some undeserved fault
Ile finde about the making of the bed,
And heere Ile fling the pillow, there the boulster,
This way the Coverlet, another way the sheets :
I, and amid this hurlie I intend,
That all is done in reverend care of her,
And in conclusion, she shal watch all night,
And if she chance to nod, Ile raile and brawle,
And with the clamor keepe her stil awake :
This is a way to kil a Wife with kindnesse,
And thus Ile curbe her mad and headstrong humor :
He that knowes better how to tame a shrew,
Now let him speake, 'tis charity to shew .

- while the speech overall is tremendously emotional (5/23 overall), reinforcing the idea of a Petruchio not in complete self-control, two unembellished lines in F #3 show a totally different spirit underlying the supposed public madman

  "I, and amid this hurlie I intend, / That all is done in reverend care of her,"

  leading into the equally unembellished

  "And in conclusion, she shal watch all night,/And if she chance to nod,"

  it might just suggest that his imposed lack of sleep is not being done maliciously, but is instead a key element in his plan, especially since the earlier unembellished line opening F #3 ('Last night she slept not, nor to night she shall not:') also refers to sleep deprivation, itself heightened by being both monosyllabic and a surround phrase

- F #1 opens highly emotionally (1/7), perhaps a suggestion that his success (by depriving Kate of any substantial food) may have taken him by surprise

- after the intellectual image (3/0 in the first three lines of F #2) of comparing his handling of Kate as to how he would a very special hawk (i.e. the 'Haggard', defined by the O.E.D as 'a wild female hawk caught in her adult plumage'; and as Ann Thompson notes in her Arden version of the play 'the purpose of training a falcon is not to break the bird's spirit'), the remainder of the speech becomes almost completely emotional (2/16 in the remaining sixteen lines)

Loves Labour's Lost

Ferdinand

Let Fame, that all hunt after in their lives,
1.1.1–23

Background: as the first speech of the play, it explains both circumstances and character.

Style: as an opener to a four-handed scene

Where: unspecified, somewhere in or close to Ferdinand's palace

To Whom: Longavile and Dumaine, out and out supporters, and, as it turns out, the somewhat doubtful Berowne

# of Lines: 23

Probable Timing: 1.10 minutes

Take Note: F's orthography reveals a King who, despite his circumspect opening, cannot contain his excitement about what he and his three friends are about to do.

Ferdinand

1   Let fame, that all hunt after in their lives,
Live regist'red upon our brazen tombs,
And then grace us in the disgrace of death ;
When spite of cormorant devouring Time,
Th'endeavor of this present breath may buy
That honor which shall bate his scythe's keen edge,
And make us heirs of all eternity .

2   Therefore, brave conquerors- for so you are,
That war against your own affections
And the huge army of the worlds desires—
Our late edict shall strongly stand in force :
Navarre shall be the wonder of the world ;
Our court shall be a little academe,
Still and contemplative in living art .

3   You three, Berowne, Dumaine, and Longaville,
Have sworn for three years' term to live with me :
My fellow scholars, and to keep those statutes
That are recorded in this schedule here .

4   Your oaths are pass'd, and now subscribe your names,
That his own hand may strike his honor down,
That violates the smallest branch herein .

5   If you are arm'd to do, as sworn to do,
Subscribe to your deep [oath], and keep it to .

Ferdinand

1   Let Fame, that all hunt after in their lives,
     Live registred upon our brazen Tombes,
     And then grace us in the disgrace of death :
     {W}hen spight of cormorant devouring Time,
     Th'endevour of this present breath may buy :
     That honour which shall bate his sythes keene edge,
     And make us heyres of all eternitie .

2   Therefore brave Conquerours, for so you are,
     That warre against your owne affections,
     And the huge Armie of the worlds desires.

3   Our late edict shall strongly stand in force,
     Navar shall be the wonder of the world .

4   Our Court shall be a little Achademe,
     Still and contemplative in living Art .

5   You three, Berowne, Dumaine, and Longavill,
     Have sworne for three yeeres terme, to live with me :
     My fellow Schollers, and to keepe thost statutes,
     That are recorded in this scedule heere .

6   Your oathes are past, and now subscribe your names :
     That his owne hand may strike his honour downe,
     That violates the smallest branch heerein :
     If you are arm'd to doe, as sworne to do,
     Subscribe to your deepe [oathes], and keepe it to .

- the three unembellished lines point to Ferdinand's deep-held long-ings and beliefs that they should not seek fame but (F #1 line three) let it

    "And then grace us in the disgrace of death : ", because

    "Our late edict shall strongly stand in force,/Navar shall be the wonder of the world."

- and the single surround phrase points to the importance of what they have done and are about to do

    " . Your oathes are past, and now subscribe your names : "

- Ferdinand begins quite carefully, the opening maxim starting intel-lectually (4/1 in the first five lines of F #1)

- the totally ungrammatical colon at the end of line five suggests that Ferdinand believes he is about to say something truly important for himself and those with him (that they will be 'heyres of all eternitie') and needs to gather himself before speaking—not surprisingly, it's at this point that emotions flood him (0/3 in the last two lines of F #1)

- but Ferdinand manfully recovers self-control, as he names the four of them 'Conquerours' of their 'owne affections' and the 'worlds desires' (F#2, 2/1), though he needs an extra breath-thought (marked ,) to do so; this is followed by F #3's unembellished (dramatically quiet?) impor-tance of 'Navar' becoming the 'wonder of the world', while the thought that his three companions will help form the 'Achademe' is almost to-tally intellectual once more (6/1, F #4 and the first line of F #5)

- and then the emotional floodgates swing wide open, calling upon them to now sign the 'scedule' as they have earlier 'sworne to do' (1/16 in the last eight lines of the speech)

Loves Labour's Lost

Berowne

The King he is hunting the Deare,
4.3.1–20

Background: though later in the play and thus the day, this is essentially a continuation of the mood of Beowne's horror-struck speech #3 above. What is interesting is that, unlike the previous speech, this switches to more immediate prose after the first two lines—perhaps suggesting that Berowne cannot be as graceful about his dilemma as he was in the earlier speech. (These first two lines refer to the fact that supposedly Ferdinand, the King, is hunting, though he appears onstage equally in love in a few moments as the 'one with a paper').

Style: solo

To Whom: direct audience address

Where: unspecified outdoors, perhaps in the gardens of or the woods beyond the palace, an area where there is one tree in which Berowne hides at the end of the speech

# of Lines: 19

Probable Timing: 1.00 minutes

Take Note: To open, F and Q set two short, possibly verse, lines, as if the enormity of the situation makes it difficult for Berowne to start talking—only the second time in the F version of the play that he is so dumb-struck. Most modern texts not only render the opening as normal, by folding the opening back into the speech, but set the whole as one continuous passage of prose, instead of allowing F and Q's verse opening to fall back into prose as the enormity hits.

Berowne

1   The King he is hunting the deer: I am coursing myself.

2   They have pitch'd a toil: I am toiling in a pitch-
     pitch that defiles—defile! a foul word .

3   Well, "set thee
     down sorrow!" for so they say the fool said, and so say
     I, and I the fool : well proved, wit !

4   By the Lord, this
     love is as mad as Ajax .

5   It kills sheep; it kills me, I a
     sheep : well proved again a my side !

6   I will not love ;
     if I do, hang me ; i'faith I will not .

7   O but her eye—by
     this light, but for her eye, I would not love her ; yes, for
     her two eyes .

8   Well, I do nothing in the world but lie,
     and lie in my throat .

9   By heaven, I do love, and it hath
     taught me to rhyme, and to be [melancholy]; and here is
     part of my rhyme, and here my [melancholy] .

10   Well, she
     hath one a'my sonnets already : the clown bore it, the
     fool sent it, and the lady hath it : sweet clown, swee-
     ter fool, sweetest lady !

11   By the world, I would not care
     a pin, if the other three were in .

12   Here comes one with a
     paper, God give him grace to groan!

Berowne

1 The King he is hunting the Deare,
I am coursing my selfe .

2 They have pitcht a Toyle, I am toyling in a pytch,
pitch that defiles ; defile, a foule word : Well, set thee
downe sorrow ; for so they say the foole said, and so say
I, and I the foole : Well proved wit .

3   By the Lord this
Love is as mad as Ajax, it kils sheepe, it kils mee, I a
sheepe : Well proved againe a my side .

4   I will not love ;:
if I do hang me : yfaith I will not .

5   O but her eye : by
this light, but for her eye, I would not love her ; yes, for
her two eyes .

6   Well, I doe nothing in the world but lye,
and lye in my throate .

7   By heaven I doe love, and it hath
taught mee to Rime, and to be [mallicholie] : and here is
part of my Rime, and heere my [mallicholie] .

8   Well, she
hath one a'my Sonnets already, the Clowne bore it, the
Foole sent it, and the Lady hath it : sweet Clowne, swee-
ter Foole, sweetest Lady .

9   By the world, I would not care
a pin, if the other three were in .

10   Here comes one with a
paper, God give him grace to grone .

- the enormity of Berowne's struggle can also be seen in the wild mood swings—the passionate opening of hunting, 'coursing my selfe' (2/2, F #1); followed immediately by the emotional recognition that he is defiling himself (1/4, the first one and a half lines of F #2, up to 'a foule word'); proving himself to be a fool several times over is passionate (6/7, the remainder of F #2 through F #4); then, the unembellished adoration of 'her eye' (F #5); returning to passion as he realises the depth of his love and therefore his 'mallicholie' (2/9, F #6-7); at last comes some intellect, still tinged with emotion, as he riffs on the word 'sweet' (F #8, 7/4); finishing with almost no energy, as if the previous part of the speech has been too much for him (F #9-10. 1/0)

- that this speech is much more disturbing than #3 above can also be seen in the first appearance of semicolons (four); the large number of possible surround phrases (eleven); and the fact that not only are there two totally unembellished sentences (the monosyllabic F #5, once more dealing with the power of 'eyes' to enchant; and the monosyllabic F #9 wishing that his three friends were similarly entrapped), but two more short sentences are also unembellished, save for one word each (the almost monosyllabic F #4, vowing he will not love and the final F #10, hoping the newcomer to the scene is one of his colleagues who will prove to be in love too)

- while the unembellished lines underscore his wishes, most of the surround phrases point to what disturbs him; ' ; defile, a foule word : Well, set thee downe sorrow : for so they say the foole said, and so say I, and I the foole : Well proved wit .' '; plus 'I will not love ; if I do hang me : yfaith I will not .' plus ' ; yes, for her two eyes .' plus ' : and here is part of my Rime, and heere my [mallicholie] .'

Loves Labour's Lost

King

Come sir, you blush : as his, your case is such,
4.3.129–148

Background: having seen Longavile hypocritically berate Dumaine for exactly the same offence Longavile has committed, (trying to contact a woman and thus breaking his oath), the King, equally hypocritically, steps forward and berates both of them, and bids them think how appallingly they would be treated if Berowne only knew…which of course he does.

Style: rebuke, as part of a three-handed scene

Where: unspecified: presumably, anywhere in the palace grounds or woods which offers bushes or trees in which the first three perjured lovers can hide to spy on the others

To Whom: Dumaine and Longavile

# of Lines: 20

Probable Timing: 1.00 minutes

Take Note: That six of the fourteen sentences are short and that five of them come when Ferdinand (the King) is either berating Longavile and Dumaine or worrying what Berowne will say, suggests how little he is able to mask his feelings.

King

1   Come, sir, you blush ; as his your case is such ;
    You chide at him, offending twice as much .

2   You do not love Maria ?

3   Longaville
    Did never sonnet for her sake compile,
    Nor never lay his wreathed arms athwart
    His loving bosom to keep down his heart .

4   I have been closely shrouded in this bush
    And mark'd you both, and for you both did blush .

5   I heard your guilty rhymes, observ'd your fashion,
    Saw sighs reek from you, noted well your passion .

6   "Ay me", says one, "O Jove", the other cries;
    [One] her hairs were gold, crystal the other's eyes .

7   You would for paradise break faith and troth,

8   And Jove for your love would infringe an oath .

9   What will Berowne say when that he shall hear
    Faith infringed, which such zeal did swear ?

10 How will he scorn ! how will he spend his wit !

11 How will he triumph, leap, and laugh at it !

12 For all the wealth that ever I did see,
    I would not have him know so much by me

King

1　Come sir, you blush : as his, your case is such,
　　You chide at him, offending twice as much .

2　You doe not love Maria ?

3　　　　　　　　　　Longavile,
　　Did never Sonnet for her sake compile ;
　　Nor never lay his wreathed armes athwart
　　His loving bosome, to keepe downe his heart .

4　I have beene closely shrowded in this bush,
　　And markt you both, and for you both did blush .

5　I heard your guilty Rimes, observ'd your fashion :
　　Saw sighes reeke from you, noted well your passion .

6　Aye me, sayes one!

7　　　　　　　　　　O Jove, the other cries!

8　[On] her haires were Gold, Christall the others eyes .

9　You would for Paradise breake Faith and troth,

10　And Jove for your Love would infringe an oath .

11　What will Berowne say when that he shall heare
　　Faith infringed which such zeale did sweare .

12　How will he scorne ? how will he spend his wit ?

13　How will he triumph, leape, and laugh at it ?

14　For all the wealth that ever I did see,
　　I would not have him know so much by me .

- Ferdinand becomes momentarily much more factual as he repeats back to them phrases from their love-sick poems 97/3, F #7-10), but then very emotional as he fears Berowne's learning of their behaviour (1/5, F #11-13), finishing with a very self-contained (concerned) un-embellished finale (F #14)

- the extreme quiet of the unembellished rebukes show what Ferdinand wishes them to believe has disturbed him (whether good hypocritical play-acting or genuine is up to each reader to decide)

  > "Come sir, you blush : as his, your case is such,/You chide at him, offending twice as much .'

  for Ferdinand has hidden

  > "…closely shrowded in this bush, /And markt you both, and for you both did blush ." & "noted well your passion"

  though from what almost immediately follows, his unembellished fear of Berowne

  > "For all the wealth that ever I did see,/I would not have him know so much by me ."

  is genuine, and, as it turns out, highly justified

- the few surround phrases suggest where Ferdinand's indignancy (whether play acting or genuine) might just get the better of him, from the opening monosyllabic ' . Come sir, you blush : ', through to the (semicolon) emotionally created ' . Longavile,/Did never Sonnet for her sake compile ; ' to the final denunciation of both of them ' . I heard your guilty Rimes, observ'd your fashion : /Saw sighes reeke from you, noted well your passion . '

- the speech starts neutrally as Ferdinand faces down Longavile (F #1), then moves into a little intellect and emotional release as he begins to detail Longavile's equally culpable love (2/1, F #2 and the first line and a half of F #3), then becomes emotional as he rips them both apart (0/9, from the last two lines of F #3 through to F #6)

Loves Labour's Lost

Berowne

Thus poure the stars down plagues for perjury .
5.2.394–418

Background: even the men's attempts to deny any knowledge of the Russian fiasco blows up as the women mock and challenge the men to confess they were the Russians. Rosaline has the bit between her teeth as she triumphantly defeats their every evasion, and in the following Berowne attempts to placate her both by confessing and promising his future wooing will be nowhere near as flamboyant in manner or language. One note: line 23, Rosaline's comment, marked {†}, has been adapted and given to Berowne so that he catches himself using a foreign language ('sans' = unnecessary flamboyance) rather than she.

Style: supposedly one on one in front of a large group

Where: close to wherever the French Ladies' private encampment is

To Whom: directly to his love Rosaline, in front of his three fellow oath-breakers, her three friends, and Boyet

# of Lines: 25

Probable Timing: 1.15 minutes

Take Note: There is a tendency for the speech to be played as if Berowne were still being glib. Yet F's sentence structure and orthography suggest that, while he may still be attempting to joke his way out of trouble, he may not be finding it quite so easy as most modern texts suggest.

Berowne

1   Thus pour the stars down plagues for perjury .

2   Can any face of brass hold longer out ?

3   Here stand I, lady dart thy skill at me,
    Bruise me with scorn, confound me with a flout,
    Thrust thy sharp wit quite through my ignorance,
    Cut me to pieces with thy keen conceit ;
    And I will wish thee never more to dance,
    Nor never more in Russian habit wait .

4   O, never will I trust to speeches penn'd,
    Nor to the motion of a schoolboys tongue,
    Nor never come in vizard to my friend,
    Nor woo in rhyme, like a blind harper's song,
    Taffeta phrases, silken terms precise,
    Three-pil'd hyperboles, spruce affection,
    Figures pedantical- these summer flies,
    Have blown me full of maggot ostentation .

5   I do forswear them, and I here protest,
    By this white glove (how white the hand, God knows!)
    Henceforth my wooing mind shall be express'd
    In russet yeas and honest kersey noes .

6   And to begin, wench, so God help me law!
    My love to thee is sound, sans crack or flaw .

7 {†} Sans, "sans", {you'll} pray {me} .

8   Yet I have a trick
    Of the old rage .

9   Bear with me, I am sick ;
    I'll leave it by degrees .

Berowne

1　Thus poure the stars down plagues for perjury .

2　Can any face of brasse hold longer out ?

3　Heere stand I, Ladie dart thy skill at me,
　　Bruise me with scorne, confound me with a flout .

4　Thrust thy sharpe wit quite through my ignorance .

5　Cut me to peeces with thy keene conceit :
　　And I will wish thee never more to dance,
　　Nor never more in Russian habit waite .

6　O! never will I trust to speeches pen'd,
　　Nor to the motion of a Schoole-boies tongue .

7　Nor never come in vizard to my friend,
　　Nor woo in rime like a blind-harpers songue,
　　Taffata phrases, silken tearmes precise,
　　Three-pil'd Hyperboles, spruce affection ;
　　Figures pedanticall, these summer flies,
　　Have blowne me full of maggot ostentation .

8　I do forsweare them, and I heere protest,
　　By this white Glove (how white the hand God knows)
　　Henceforth my woing minde shall be exprest
　　In russet yeas, and honest kersie noes .

9　And to begin Wench, so God helpe me law,
　　My love to thee is sound, sans cracke or flaw .

10 {†} Sans, sans, {you'll} pray {me} .

11　　　　　　　　　　　　　　Yet I have a tricke
　　Of the old rage : beare with me, I am sicke .

12　Ile leave it by degrees :

- three of the first four sentences are short, suggesting he cannot immediately access his customary elaborate word spinning abilities

- also the first surround phrase opening F #5 ' . Cut me to peeces with thy keene conceit : ' could suggest the invitation has more bite to it than might at first be expected

- and in finishing, once he realises he has fallen into the trap of word-play yet again, the last threes sentences are short, perhaps suggesting that there is some sincerity to the apology, especially considering sentences F #11-12 are also formed by surround phrases ' . Yet I have a tricke/Of the old rage : beare with me, I am sicke . / Ile leave it by degrees : '

- it also seems that Berowne is taking great care to advance his argument detailed step by step, far more so than his modern counterpart, for, in first inviting Rosaline to mock him, and in decrying his former behaviour, whereas most modern texts set just two sentences (mt. #3-4), F allows him five sentences to make the same points (F #3-7)

- the speech opening himself to attack starts quite emotionally (2/8 in the eight lines of F #1-5)

- Berowne's start to denying any future similar foolish behaviour becomes passionate (5/6, F #6 and the first four lines of F #7), but he turns again to emotion as he forswears any further elaborate language (0/4 in the last two lines of F #7 and the first line of F #8)

- and in starting his new linguistic form he becomes passionate once again (4/4 in the last three lines of F #8 plus F #9), only to waver between the (deliberate?) calm of non-embellishment (F #10 and #12) and emotion (0/3, F #11) once the short sentences begin

- the colon ending the speech suggests that Berowne interrupts himself as he sees the reactions of his fellow oath-breakers to his speech

A Midsommer Nights Dreame

Lysander

I am my Lord, as well deriv'd as he,
1.1.99–110

Background: Egeus has chosen Demetrius (a 'Lordship') as husband for his daughter, Hermia, even though Demetrius has been involved with the other young Athenian woman in the play, Helena. However, Lysander and Hermia are in love. This, Lysander's first major speech in the play, is self-explanatory.

Style: public statement

Where: somewhere in Theseus' palace

To Whom: Duke Theseus, in front of the rival Demetrius; Hermia's father, Egeus; Hermia; and Hippolita; perhaps with court officials also in attendance, though none are indicated in the original stage directions.

# of Lines: 12

Probable Timing: 0.40 minutes

Take Note: Though Lysander is often portrayed as a brash young man, here F seems to that suggest he is being very careful in justifying his actions—possibly aware of both the seriousness of the situation and the need for decorum in front of the Duke.

Lysander

1   I am, my Lord, as well deriv'd as he,
    As well possess'd; my love is more [than] his ;
    My fortunes every way as fairly rank'd
    (If not with vantage) as Demetrius ;
    And (which is more [than] all these boasts can be)
    I am belov'd of beauteous Hermia .

2   Why should not I then prosecute my right ?

3   Demetrius, I'll avouch it to his head,
    Made love to Nedar's daughter, Helena,
    And won her soul; and she, sweet Lady, dotes,
    Devoutly dotes, dotes in idolatry,
    Upon this spotted and inconstant man .

Lysander

1 I am my Lord, as well deriv'd as he,
   As well possest : my love is more [then] his :
   My fortunes every way as fairely ranck'd
   (If not with vantage) as Demetrius :
   And (which is more [then] all these boasts can be)
   I am belov'd of beauteous Hermia .

2 Why should not I then prosecute my right ?

3 Demetrius, Ile avouch it to his head,
   Made love to Nedars daughter, Helena,
   And won her soule : and she (sweet Ladie)dotes,
   Devoutly dotes, dotes in Idolatry,
   Upon this spotted and inconstant man .

- as a whole, the speech is highly factual and self-contained (8/2 over-all), with no fewer than four logical colons, with the one surround phrase clearly pointing to his belief that he is behaving fairly, ': my love is more than his : ', doubly heightened by being both monosyllabic and unembellished

- this is supported by F #2, the only short sentence, again unembellished,

    "Why should not I then prosecute my right?"

- and even his exposition of Demetrius' unfaithfulness is summarised with great care, via the final unembellished statement that Helena

    "dotes/Devoutly dotes…/Upon this spotted and inconstant man."

A Midsommer Nights Dreame

Lysander

Transparent Helena, nature her shewes art,
between 2.2.103–122

Background: Oberon, taking pity on the abandoned Helena, has ordered Puck to enchant Demetrius' eyes so that he will fall in love with her when he wakes. He didn't realise that two Athenian men were in the woods that night and told Puck to find the man by the 'Athenian garments he hath on', so, Puck correctly zaps a man wearing Athenian garments. Unfortunately it's Lysander, not Demetrius, who awakes, spies Helena, and, as the power of the charm demands, falls immediately in love with her. He thus begins to woo her as ardently as he possibly can. With Helena having run away, Lysander abandons his once-loved Hermia and vows he will be a chivalric figure for Helena and become 'her Knight'.

Style: a two handed scene

Where: somewhere in the wood

To Whom: to Helena, who then runs off in dismay

# of Lines: 14

Probable Timing: 0.45 minutes

Take Note: F's orthography clearly shows that Lysander's struggles to put some logic in the emotional turmoil of his new found/magically induced adoration, for the speech veers rapidly between emotion, intellect and, a single moment of unembellished self-control, all within just fourteen lines of heightened rhyming couplets.

Lysander

1   Transparent Helena, nature [shows her art],
     That through thy bosom makes me see thy heart .

---

2   Content with Hermia ?

3   No; I do repent
     The tedious minutes I with her have spent .

4   Not Hermia, but Helena [ ] I love .

5   Who will not change a raven for a dove ?

6   The will of man is by his reason sway'd ;
     And reason says you are the worthier maid .

7   Things growing are not ripe until their season,
     So, I being young, till now ripe not to reason ;
     And touching now the point of [human] skill,
     Reason becomes the marshal to my will,
     And leads me to your eyes, where I o'erlook
     Loves stories written in Love's richest book .

Lysander

1   Transparent Helena, nature [her shewes art],-
    That through thy bosome makes me see thy heart .

---

2   Content with Hermia ?

3   No, I do repent
    The tedious minutes I with her have spent .

4   Not Hermia, but Helena [now] I love ;
    Who will not change a Raven for a Dove ?

5   The will of man is by his reason sway'd :
    And reason saies you are the worthier Maide .

6   Things growing are not ripe untill their season ;
    So I being yong, till now ripe not to reason,
    And touching now the point of [humane] skill,
    Reason becomes the Marshall to my will,
    And leades me to your eyes, where I orelooke
    Loves stories, written in Loves richest booke .

- the first sight of Helena awakes his (initially tongue stumbling) emotions (1/2, F #1), which prompts him to move into a mix of intellect (F #2 and #4, 5/0) and non-embellishment (F #3) as he puts Hermia quite out of his mind

- and then the chop-logic finale (an illogical bending of words and/or ideas to prove something that cannot actually be proven) turns highly emotional (3/7, F #5-6)

- the final long-spelling rhyming couplet ('orelooke', 'booke') underscores that he finally believes the chop-logic illogicality he has offered to prove that though once betrothed to Hermia (when 'yong'), now he is mature ('ripe to reason'), he is free to put Hermia aside so as to woo Helena

- the underlying struggle between emotion and intellect can be seen in the surround phrases, for the on-the-surface intellectual F #4 rejection of Hermia is comprised of two surround phrases created by the emotional semicolon, while the two surround phrases of F #5's emotional ending statement of Helena's worth are created by a logical colon

A Midsommer Nights Dreame

Demetrius

My Lord, faire Helen told me of their stealth,
4.1.160–176

Background: To Egeus' horror, the royal hunting party have discovered side by side Demetrius with Helena and Lysander with Hermia. Triggered by an anguished plea from Egeus that the full impact of the law be visited upon Lysander, this is Demetrius' response.

Style: direct address involving two people as part of a larger scene

Where: somewhere in the woods

To Whom: Duke Theseus, also Helena, and probably the others immediately involved in his discovery, notably Hermia, Lysander and Egeus; also present is Hippolita, and perhaps members of Theseus' retinue

# of Lines: 17

Probable Timing: 0.55 minutes

Take Note: much critical anguish has been expressed over this speech, stemming from the fact that, for Demetrius to be still in love with Helena, as he was forced to be when enchanted, the spell must not have been removed from his eyes as it was from Lysander's. However, Demetrius' rarely used early quarto comment to Helena 'I do not, NOT I cannot love you' can resolve this current speech's awkwardness: unfortunately, most modern texts follow the First Folio and have Demetrius say earlier 'I do not, NOR I cannot love you'—a much nastier and more awkward comment.

Demetrius

1   My Lord, fair Helen told me of their stealth,
Of this their purpose hither, to this wood,
And I in fury hither followed them,
Fair Helena in fancy [following] me .

2   But, my good Lord, I wot not by what power
(But by some power it is), my love to Hermia
(Melted as the snow) seems to me now
As the remembrance of an idle gaud,
Which in my childhood I did dote upon ;
And all the faith, the virtue of my heart,
The object and the pleasure of [my] eye,
Is only Helena .

3   To her, my Lord,
Was I betrothed ere I [saw] Hermia ;
But like a sickness did I loathe this food ;
But, as in health, come to my natural taste,
Now [I do] wish it, love it, long for it,
And will for evermore be true to it .

Demetrius

1   My Lord, faire Helen told me of their stealth,
     Of this their purpose hither, to this wood,
     And I in furie hither followed them ;
     Faire Helena, in fancy [followed] me .

2   But my good Lord, I wot not by what power,
     (But by some power it is) my love
     To Hermia (melted as the snow)
     Seems to me now as the remembrance of an idle gaude,
     Which in my childehood I did doat upon :
     And all the faith, the vertue of my heart,
     The object and the pleasure of [mine] eye,
     Is onely Helena .

3   To her, my Lord,
     Was I betroth'd, ere I [see] Hermia,
     But like a sickenesse did I loath this food,
     But as in health, come to my naturall taste,
     Now [doe I] wish it, love it, long for it,
     And will for evermore be true to it .

- the speech starts out passionately (F #1 3/2), though fascinatingly the two long spellings both are in praise of 'faire' Helen/Helena

- the discovery of true love explanation starts out factually (2/0 the first three lines of F #2), both capitals referring to names or titles, then becomes emotional (1/4 the remainder of F #2)

- and F #3's self-blame summary follows a similar pattern (2/0 the first line and a half, 0/3 to finish)

- while the unembellished explanation that Helena

    "…told me of their stealth,/Of this their purpose hither, to this wood,/And I in furie hither followed them'

    may be expected as a circumspect acknowledegement both of the status of the Duke and of the bombshell he is about to drop on Egeus

- however, the similarly unembellished, essentially quiet, statement of his love (allowing for the capitalised names and titles) is not

    "But my good Lord, I wot not by what power, /(But by some power it is) my love/To Hermia (melted as the snow)/…/And all the faith, the vertue of my heart,/The object and the pleasure of mine eye,"

    "To her, my Lord,/Was I betroth'd, ere I [see] Hermia, "

    "…I wish it, love it, long for it,/And will for evermore be true to it ."

The Merchant of Venice

Bassanio

In Belmont is a Lady richly left,
1.1.161–176

Background: as Bassanio's response to Anthonio's requests for information: this is his final revelation of all the details of the lady in question, Portia, in response to Anthonio's rather naked plea 'therefore speake'.

Style: all three speeches as part of a two-handed scene

Where: unspecified

To Whom: Anthonio, to whom Bassanio is already financially indebted

# of Lines: 16

Probable Timing: 0.50 minutes

Take Note: Modern texts suggest far more self control than F establishes, this time by splitting F's onrushed opening sentence into four.

Bassanio

1   In Belmont is a lady richly left,
     And she is fair and, fairer then that word,
     Of wondrous virtues.

2   Sometimes from her eyes
     I did receive faire speechless messages .

3   Her name is Portia, nothing undervalu'd
     To Cato's daughter, Brutus' Portia .

4   Nor is the wide world ignorant of her worth,
     For the four winds blow in from every coast
     Renowned suitors, and her sunny locks
     Hang on her temples like a golden fleece,
     Which makes her seat of Belmont [Colchis'] strond,
     And many Jasons come in quest of her .

5   O my Antonio, had I but the means
     To hold a rival place with one of them,
     I have a mind presages me such thrift
     That I should questionless be fortunate !

Bassanio

1   In Belmont is a Lady richly left,
And she is faire, and fairer then that word,
Of wondrous vertues, sometimes from her eyes
I did receive faire speechlesse messages :
Her name is Portia, nothing undervallewd
To Cato's daughter, Brutus Portia,
Nor is the wide world ignorant of her worth,
For the foure windes blow in from every coast
Renowned sutors, and her sunny locks
Hang on her temples like a golden fleece,
Which makes her seat of Belmont [Cholchos] strond,
And many Jasons come in quest of her .

2   O my Anthonio, had I but the meanes
To hold a rivall place with one of them,
I have a minde presages me such thrift,
That I should questionlesse be fortunate .

- with ten capitals overall, it seems that Bassanio finally establishes some form of mental discipline for himself: however, with four of them occurring in just two lines (as he first describes Portia) plus only one piece of major punctuation in the piece, it seems it is the images of Portia (and ensuing classical ones of the quest) that are guiding him, rather than a sustained act of logical presentation of information

- while there are ten long-spelled words, they tend to come in three clusters (the 'faire speechlesse messages' he received from her; rival suitors coming from everywhere on the 'foure windes', and the final F #2 indirect plea for more money), suggesting a struggle as to when the mind is in control and when the emotions

- thus in the opening line his mind works (2/0), then for the next three his emotions (0/3): then, as he mentions Portia's name his mind takes over again (4/1) but just for two lines: then there is a period of relative calm (just 2 long spelled words in four lines) followed by a final flourish of three capitals in the last two classical analogy lines of the sentence—all this is encompassed in F #1, the overly-long sentence suggesting a see-saw battle within him, a totally different opening to that offered by modern texts

- with its four long spelled words, F #2 reverts once more to something of the emotional blurt of the previous speech

The Merchant of Venice

Lorenzo

How sweet the moone-light sleepes upon this banke,
5.1.54–68

Background: looking after Portia's home in Belmont, having been told that both Portia and Nerrissa, and Bassanio and Gratiano with the saved Anthonio, will be returning soon independently of each other, the now married Lorenzo and Jessica (Shylocke's daughter) are enjoying a final moment of togetherness before the hustle of the returning groups envelops them. These two successive speeches are Lorenzo's longest in the play; this speech is self explanatory

Style: part of a two-handed scene

Where: outdoors, perhaps a terrace or garden, part of Portia's palace

To Whom: Jessica

# of Lines: 15

Probable Timing: 0.50 minutes

Take Note: With its one sentence, F seems to suggest that Lorenzo never stops talking (whether he is enchanted by the music, the night, and his beloved, or is merely a talkative bore is up to each actor to explore). The modern texts split the speech into six grammatically correct sentences, perhaps emphasising the potential for boredom above all else.

Lorenzo

1   How sweet the moonlight sleeps upon this bank!
Here will we sit, and let the sounds of music
Creep in our ears.

2   Soft stillness and the night
Become the touches of sweet harmony .

3   Sit Jessica .

4   Look how the floor of heaven
Is thick inlaid with patens of bright gold .

5   There's not the smallest orb which thou behold'st
But in his motion like an angel sings,
Still quiring to the young-ey'd cherubins ;
Such harmony is in immortal souls,
But whilst this muddy vesture of decay
Doth grossly close [it in], we cannot hear it .

6   Come ho, and wake Diana with a hymn,
With sweetest touches pierce your mistress' ear,
And draw her home with music .

Lorenzo

1   How sweet the moone-light sleepes upon this banke,
Heere will we sit, and let the sounds of musicke
Creepe in our eares soft stilnes, and the night
Become the tutches of sweet harmonie :
Sit Jessica, looke how the floore of heaven
Is thicke inlayed with pattens of bright gold,
There's not the smallest orbe which thou beholdst
But in his motion like an Angell sings,
Still quiring to the young eyed Cherubins ;
Such harmonie is in immortall soules,
But whilst this muddy vesture of decay
Doth grosly close [in it], we cannot heare it :
Come hoe, and wake Diana with a hymne,
With sweetest tutches pearce your Mistresse eare,
And draw her home with musicke .

- this is very much a speech of personal belief rather than an intellectual thesis (only 4 capitals as opposed to 24 long spellings in just 15 lines)

- his enthusiasm seems to come in two emotional bursts, the first focusing on the 'moone-light' and 'the floore of heaven' (1/12 in the first six lines), and the instructions for the musicians to play so as to please and awaken mythical Diana and speed Portia's return home (1/7 the last three lines)

- apart from the proper name 'Jessica', the other three capitals seem to suggest a love of things mystical and mythical, viz. 'Angell'; 'Cherubins'; and the allusion to the classical goddess of chastity and the hunt, 'Diana', also a name for the moon

- there is only one phrase in the speech where there is no embellishment, and it deals with the rather darker side of the human condition,

   "But whilst this muddy vesture of decay/Doth grosly close [it in],"

The Merchant of Venice

Lorenzo

The reason is, your spirits are attentive :
5.1.70–88

Background: Following on Lorenzo's previous speech, this one is triggered by Jessica's remark, offered as music is heard from offstage, 'I am never merry when I heare sweet musique.'

Style: part of a two-handed scene

Where: outdoors, perhaps a terrace or garden, part of Portia's palace

To Whom: Jessica

# of Lines: 19

Probable Timing: 1.00 minutes

Take Note: Though the modern texts almost maintain F's sentence pattern, the seemingly minor and highly grammatical restructuring of the end of sentence #1 suppresses Lorenzo's inarticulate wonder at the power of music, and replaces it with normal rationality.

Lorenzo

1   The reason is, your spirits are attentive ;
For do but note a wild and wanton herd
Or race of youthful and unhandled colts,
Fetching mad bounds, bellowing and neighing loud,
Which is the hot condition of their blood,
If they but hear perchance a trumpet sound,
Or any air of music touch their ears,
You shall perceive them make a mutual stand,
Their savage eyes turn'd to a modest gaze,
By the sweet power of music ; therefore the poet
Did feign that Orpheus drew trees, stones, and floods ;
Since nought so stockish, hard, and full of rage,
But music for time doth change his nature .

2   The man that hath no music in himself,
Nor is not moved with concord of sweet sounds,
Is fit for treasons, stratagems, and spoils;
The motions of his spirit are dull as night,
And his affections dark as [Erebus],
Let no such man be trusted .

3   Mark the music

Lorenzo

1   The reason is, your spirits are attentive :
    For doe but note a wilde and wanton heard
    Or race of youthful and unhandled colts,
    Fetching mad bounds, bellowing and neighing loud,
    Which is the hot condition of their bloud,
    If they but heare perchance a trumpet sound,
    Or any ayre of musicke touch their eares,
    You shall perceive them make a mutuall stand,
    Their savage eyes turn'd to a modest gaze,
    By the sweet power of musicke : therefore the Poet
    Did faine that Orpheus drew trees, stones, and floods .

2   Since naught so stockish, hard, and full of rage,
    But musicke for time doth change his nature,
    The man that hath no musicke in himselfe,
    Nor is not moved with concord of sweet sounds,
    Is fit for treasons, stratagems, and spoyles,
    The motions of his spirit are dull as night,
    And his affections darke as [Erobus],
    Let no such man be trusted : marke the musicke .

- this speech, though still highly personal, is somewhat less passionate than speech #14 above (here 3/18 in eighteen lines, compared to the earlier 4/24 in fifteen)

- this could be partially because here Lorenzo's love of music seems to generate moments of total calm and/or non-embellished concentration as he explains its powers , from the opening surround phrase

   " . The reason is, your spirits are attentive : "

 'attentive' meaning 'concentrated', going on to explain music's appeal to nearly everyone

   "Since naught so stockish, hard, and full of rage,"

   "Or race of youthful and unhandled colts,/Fetching mad bounds, bellowing and neighing loud,"

 and that anyone not so moved is not to be trusted

   "Nor is not moved with concord of sweet sounds,/Is fit for treasons, stratagems…"

- even so, there is only one really emotional outburst as he describes how the 'rough and unhandled colts' can be charmed by music (0/7, six and a half lines from the fifth line 'Which is the hot condition of their bloud,'): and from this springs the one intellectual (capitalised) cluster, embracing once more the classical/mythical with the surround phrase ' : therefore the Poet/Did faine that Orpheus drew trees, stones, and floods . ', with the power of his lute (2/1)

- the final phrase, surround as it also is, reinforces his all-encompassing pre-occupation ' : marke the musicke . '

Much Adoe About Nothing

Benedicke

I noted {†} not {the daughter of signior Leonato },
but I lookt on her .
between 1.1.164–203

Background: Benedicke has been his usual somewhat crusty public self in response to Claudio's obvious attraction to and questioning about Hero.

Style: as part of a two-handed scene

Where: at Leonato's where Don Pedro's party first arrived, though indoors or outdoors is unspecified

To Whom: the smitten Claudio

# of Lines: 18

Probable Timing: 0.55 minutes

Take Note: F's orthography and sentence structure suggest that vis-a-vis Beatrice, Benedicke makes an interesting Freudian slip.

Benedicke

1   I noted {#} not {the daughter of signior Leonato },
    but I look'd on her .

---

2   Do you question me, as an honest man should
    do, for my simple true judgment ? or would you have
    me speak after my custom, as being a professed tyrant
    to their sex ?

---

3   {#} I'faith me thinks she's too low for a [high]
    praise, too brown for a fair praise, and too little for a
    great praise; only this commendation I can afford her,
    that were she other [than] she is, she were unhandsome,
    and being no other, but as she is, I do not like her .

---

4   There's her cousin, and she were not possess'd
    with a fury, exceeds her as much in beauty as the first
    of May doth the last of December .

5   But I hope you have
    no intent to turn husband, have you ?

---

6   In faith, hath not the world one
    man but he will wear his cap with suspicion ?

7   Shall I ne-
    ver see a batchelor of three score again ?

8   Go to, i'faith,
    and thou wilt needs thrust thy neck into a yoke, wear
    the print of it, and sigh away Sundays .

9   Look, Don Pedro
    is returned to seek you .

Benedicke

1   I noted {t} not {the daughter of signior Leonato },
but I lookt on her .

---

2   Doe you question me as an honest man should
doe, for my simple true judgement ? or would you have
me speake after my custome, as being a professed tyrant
to their sexe ?

---

3   {t} Yfaith me thinks shee's too low for a [hie]
praise, too browne for a faire praise, and too little for a
great praise, onely this commendation I can affoord her,
that were shee other [then] she is, she were unhandsome,
and being no other, but as she is, I doe not like her .

---

4   There's her cosin, and she were not possest
with a furie, exceedes her as much in beautie, as the first
of Maie doth the last of December : but I hope you have
no intent to turne husband, have you ?

---

5   In faith hath not the world one
man but he will weare his cap with suspition ? shall I never see a batcheller of three score againe ? goe to yfaith,
and thou wilt needes thrust thy necke into a yoke, weare
the print of it, and sigh away sundaies : looke, don Pedro
is returned to seeke you .

- the speech starts out so casually (0/1, F #1), it's almost as if Benedicke might not be paying much attention

- and then, even before he realises Claudio may be serious about Hero, the emotional releases associated with his (Benedicke's) being a 'professed tyrant' towards women start to flow (0/14 in the eight lines F #2-3)

- very interestingly, his unasked for praise of Beatrice's beauty as 'the first of Maie' is offered fairly straightforwardly (2/1, the first two lines of F #4), as if the facts were sufficient to speak for themselves—though it's interesting that the one long spelled word 'exceedes' adds extra weight to his assessment of Beatrice's 'beautie'

- the end of F #3, the hope that Claudio 'has no intent to turn husband', is usually set as a separate sentence by most modern texts, but this is a shame, for F's ungrammatical fast-link setting via the colon suggests Benedicke is nowhere near as controlled as most modern texts would have him—and, in fact, the surround phrase question may be his attempt to make a quick face-saving recovery from his Freudian slip over his out-of-place praising of Beatrice's 'beautie'—a slip perhaps heightened by the short spellings that suddenly appear associated with Beatrice, 'cosin', 'possest', 'furie', beautie', and 'Maie'

- and whether 'recovery' or no, the remainder of the speech is handled emotionally throughout (1/12 the last line of F #4 and all of F #5, six lines in all)

Much Adoe About Nothing
Benedicke

Shall I speake a word in your eare ?
between 5.1.143–193

Background: moved both by his love for Beatrice and her passionate defense of Hero, Benedicke has decided not only to part company with the Prince and thus Claudio, but to challenge Claudio to a duel; hence the following, in which he first offers the challenge. The remainder of the speech is self-explanatory, save for the comment of Pedro and Claudio having 'kill'd a sweet and innocent Ladie'—Hero is not dead, though Benedicke and the family have agreed they must publicly behave as if she is.

Style: as part of a three-handed scene

Where: unspecified, presumably in a public place

To Whom: Claudio, and then Don Pedro

# of Lines: 14

Probable Timing: 0.45 minutes

Take Note: Given the circumstances, here there are very few passages of sustained emotion—very surprising when compared to his previous high release

Benedicke

1   Shall I speak a word in your ear ?

―――――――――――――――――――――――――――――――

2   You are a villain .

3   I jest not, I will make it good
       how you dare, with what you dare, and when you dare .

4   Do me right, or I will protest your cowardice .

5   You have
       kill'd a sweet lady, and her death shall fall heavy on
       you .

6   Let me hear from you .

―――――――――――――――――――――――――――――――

7   Fare you well, boy, you know my mind .

8   I will
       leave you now to your gossip-like humor .

9   You break
       jests as braggards do their blades, which, God be thank'd,
       hurt not .

10   My Lord, for your many courtesies I thank
       you .

11   I must discontinue your company .

12   Your brother
       the bastard is fled from Messina .

13   You have among you,
       kill'd a sweet and innocent lady .

14   For my Lord Lack
       beard there, he and I shall meet, and till then peace be
       with him .

Benedicke

1   Shall I speake a word in your eare ?

---

2   You are a villaine, I jest not, I will make it good
how you dare, with what you dare, and when you dare :
do me right, or I will protest your cowardise : you have
kill'd a sweete Ladie, and her death shall fall heavie on
you, let me heare from you .

---

3   Fare you well, Boy, you know my minde, I will
leave you now to your gossep-like humor, you breake
jests as braggards do their blades, which God be thank-
ed hurt not : my Lord, for your manie courtesies I thank
you, I must discontinue your companie, your brother
the Bastard is fled from Messina : you have among you,
kill'd a sweet and innocent Ladie : for my Lord Lacke-
beard there, he and I shall meete, and till then peace be
with him .

- the opening short emotional sentence is the first hint as to how difficult this challenge to a one-time friend and subsequent withdrawal from his patron's service and protection is going to be (0/2)

- Benedicle's internal struggle is beautifully suggested by the fact that though F #2 is onrushed, there is, for him, very little release therein (1/3 in four and a half lines)

- similarly, though F #3 opens passionately (2/3 in the first three lines plus), the withdrawal from Don Pedro's company, news of his brother's flight, and simple statement that they are responsible for Hero's death, all are handled without passion (3/0 the next four lines)—though the intellectual control is joined by emotion for the final belittling reminder of the challenge to Claudio (2/2 the last two lines)

- the two surround phrases point to how serious Benedicke now is

    " : do me right, or I will protest your cowardise : "

    " : you have among you, kill'd a sweet and innocent Ladie : "

    both of which are further heightened by being unembellished icily-calm

- and the one remaining section of unembellished lines shows that this is not time for casual excess, for Benedicke has this to say about Claudio's being a 'villaine'

    "I jest not, I will make it good how you dare, with what you dare, and when you dare:"

    the monosyllables of the challenge heightened by being followed with the first surround phrase set above

The Merry Wives of Windsor

Slender

Whoa hoe, hoe, Father Page .
between 5.5.177–193

Background: in a complex series of plottings to take place at the same time as the tricking of Falstaffe, Mistris Page arranged for daughter Anne to be dressed in one colour so Caius could recognise her and steal her away to be quickly married while, unbeknownst to his wife, Master Page has arranged for Anne to be in a different colour so Slender could recognise her and steal her away to be quickly married instead. As it turns out Anne manages to trick everyone and marry Fenton (of whom neither parent approves). Here the dismayed Slender tells of his embarrassing failure. One note: F#5/mt.#6 have been inserted here from later in the speech to allow Master Slender a more logical explanation.

Style: one on one in front of a larger group

Where: at 'Herne the Hunter's Oake' in Windsor Forest

To Whom: to Page, in front of Falstaffe, the assembled company of Mistris Quickly, Pistoll, Evans and various children and young people, all disguised as Fairies, the watching Fords and Mistris Page

# of Lines: 13

Probable Timing: 0.45 minutes

Slender

1   Whoa ho, ho! father Page .

---

2   {I am not d}ispatch'd {!}

3   I'll make the best in Gloucestershire
    know on't .

4   Would I were hang'd la, else !

---

5   I came yonder at Eton to marry Mistress Anne
    Page, and she's a great lubberly boy .

---

6   I went to her in [white], and cried "mum", and
    she cried "budget", as Anne and I had appointed, and yet
    it was not Anne, but a postmaster's boy .

---

7   If it had not been
    i'th church, I would have swing'd him, or he should
    have swing'd me .

8   If I did not think it had been Anne
    Page, would I might never stir! and 'tis a postmaster's
    boy .

---

9   If I had been married to him,
    (for all he was in woman's apparel) I would not have
    had him .

Slender

1   Whoa hoe, hoe, Father Page .

---

2   {I am not d}ispatch'd {!}

3   Ile make the best in Glostershire
     know on't :would I were hang'd la, else .

---

4   I came yonder at Eaton to marry Mistris Anne
     Page, and she's a great lubberly boy .

---

5   I went to her in [greene], and cried Mum, and
     she cride budget, as Anne and I had appointed, and yet
     it was not Anne, but a Post-masters boy .

---

6   If it had not bene
     i'th Church, I would have swing'd him, or hee should
     have swing'd me .

7   If I did not thinke it had been Anne
     Page, would I might never stirre, and 'tis a Post-masters
     Boy .

---

8   If I had bene married to him,
     (for all he was in womans apparrell) I would not have
     had him .

- after a wonderful opening running-on-stage verbal explosion (2/3, the short F #1), Slender, at least momentarily, manages to restore himself to a sense of dignity for the dreadful news for himself and Anne's father that he is not married (1/0, F #2-3)

- indeed, the further explanation of how the girl he thought he had married, despite being dressed in 'greene' and their exchanging the agreed upon pass-words 'Mum' and 'budget', has turned out to be a 'lubberly boy' (F #4-5) is a surprising mix of facts (8/1 in just five lines) and (including phrases from F #2-3 too) unembellished dignity preserving comments

    "I am not dispatch'd" plus "would I were hang'd la else"

    "and she's a great lubberly boy"

- and, for almost the first time in the play, he seems determined to take some sort of stand, for the whole of sentence two

    " . Ile make the best in Glostershire know on't : would I were hang'd la, else . "

  is made up of unembellished surround phrases

- but the control and intellect do not last, for informing all that it was only the discovery of the mistake being revealed in a church that prevented fisticuffs, followed by the fairly obvious statement that he wouldn't have married a 'Post-masters Boy' instead of Anne Page had he known, becomes passionate (5/5, F #6-7)

- while the final reassertion 'I would not have had him.' becomes almost self-controlled once more (just 0/1 in the two lines of F #8)

As You Like It

Orlando

As I remember Adam, it was upon this fashion
1.1.1–25

Background: the first speech of the play, explaining the appalling relationship between Orlando de Boys and Oliver, his oldest brother, the inheritor of the estate of their recently deceased father. As such it is self explanatory.

Style: as part of a two-handed scene **Where:** the orchard of the de Boys family **To Whom:** Adam, the nearly eighty year old family retainer, loyal to Orlando

# of Lines: 24

Probable Timing: 1.15 minutes

Take Note: Though the structures match at the end of the speech, and though Orlando manages to reach a state of self-control by the time he's finished, the Folio & modern openings of the speech are totally different, with F's Orlando having one of the longest onrushed first sentences in Shakespeare—F's whole suggesting a gigantic outburst at the start of the play which he manages to control by speech's end.

Orlando

1   As I remember, Adam, it was upon this fashion
    bequeathed me by will but poor a thousand
    crowns, and, as thou say'st, charged my bro-
    ther, on his blessing, to breed me well ; and
    there begins my sadness .

2   My brother Jacques he keeps
    at school, and report speaks goldenly of his profit .

3   For my part, he keeps me rustically at home, or (to speak
    more properly) stays me here at home unkept ; for call
    you that keeping for a gentleman of my birth, that dif-
    fers not from the stalling of an ox ?

4   His horses are bred
    better, for besides that they are fair with their feeding,
    they are taught their manage, and to that end riders
    dearly hir'd ; but I (his brother) gain nothing under
    him but growth, for the which his animals on his
    dunghills are as much bound to him as I .

5   Besides this no-
    thing that he so plentifully gives me, the something that
    nature gave me his countenance seems to take from
    me .

6   He lets me feed with his hinds, bars me the
    place of a brother, and as much as in him lies, mines my
    gentility with my education .

7   This is it, Adam, that
    grieves me, and the spirit of my father, which I think
    is within me, begins to mutiny against this servitude .

8   I will no longer endure it, though yet I know no wise
    remedy how to avoid it .

Orlando

1   As I remember Adam, it was upon this fashion
bequeathed me by will, but poore a thousand
Crownes, and as thou saist, charged my brother on his blessing to breed mee well :and
there begins my sadnesse : My brother Jacques he keepes
at schoole, and report speakes goldenly of his profit :
for my part, he keepes me rustically at home, or (to speak
more properly) staies me heere at home unkept :for call
you that keeping for a gentleman of my birth, that dif-
fers not from the stalling of an Oxe ? his horses are bred
better, for besides that they are faire with their feeding,
they are taught their mannage, and to that end Riders
deerely hir'd : but I (his brother) gaine nothing under
him but growth, for the which his Animals on his
dunghils are as much bound to him as I : besides this nothing that he so plentifully gives me, the something that
nature gave mee, his countenance seemes to take from
me : hee lets mee feede with his Hindes, barres mee the
place of a brother, and as much as in him lies, mines my
gentility with my education .

2   This is it Adam that
grieves me, and the spirit of my Father, which I thinke
is within mee, begins to mutinie against this servitude .

3   I will no longer endure it, though yet I know no wise
remedy how to avoid it .

- the opening of the speech, setting out the details of the will and how the middle brother Jacques is well taken care of by older brother and inheritor of the state Oliver, is, quite naturally, passionate (6/6 in the first six lines)

- as the surround phrases suggest, the root of the trouble stems from Oliver's refusal to carry out certain provisions of his father's will, at least as regards Orlando

  " : and there begins my sadnesse : My brother Jacques he keepes at schoole, and report speakes goldenly of his profit : "

- and as Orlando goes on to detail his ill-treatment the speech turns emotional, at first under a fair amount of control (3/9 in ten lines), but, as he describes how he has to 'feede with his Hindes' (his brother's farm-labourers), he finally explodes (1/6 in just one line), and then he regains control for the last line and a half of F #1

- there is a moment of passion again (2/2, F #2) as he invokes the spirit of 'my Father' (2/2) to justify his possible 'mutinie against this servitude'

- thus, given the orthography of the opening to the speech, remarkably he manages to re-establish complete self-control for the last sentence

- throughout, the unembellished lines point to the uncomfortable details past, present, and even future that have and continue to give Orlando great difficulties in resolving

  "it was upon this fashion bequeathed me by will,"

  "for call you that keeping for a gentleman of my birth", i.e.

  "besides this nothing that he so plentifully gives me",

  "and as much as in him lies, mines my gentility with my education"

  so that Orlando's spirit, shaped by that of his recently deceased father

  "begins to mutinie against this servitude. I will no longer endure it, though yet I know no wise remedy how to avoid it."

As You Like It

Oliver

Charles, I thanke thee for thy love to me,
1.1.137–158

Background: just before Charles' arrival, the two brothers came to blows, ending with Orlando nearly throttling Oliver and then demanding the small inheritance granted by his father's will. Oliver has essentially vowed revenge ('I will physicke your ranknesse'). Charles' news seems heaven sent, and thus Oliver begins to inflame Charles so that he will look forward to injuring Orlando in the ring.

Style: as part of a two-handed scene

Where: the orchard of the de Boys family

To Whom: Charles, the Duke's wrestler

# of Lines: 19

Probable Timing: 1.00 minutes

Take Note: Despite the high emotion of the speech (3/27 in just nineteen lines), Oliver seems to be exhibiting great skill in the manipulation of Charles—the quiet unembellished lines seem superbly designed to awake Charles' mistrust towards Orlando prior to the wrestling.

Oliver

1　Charles, I thank thee for thy love to me, which
thou shalt find I will most kindly requite .

2　　　　　　　　　　　　　　　　　　I had my
self notice of my Brothers purpose herein, and have by
underhand means labor'd to dissuade him from it ;
but he is resolute .

3　　　　　　　　　　　　I'll tell thee, Charles, it is the stubbornest young fellow of France, full of ambition, an envious
emulator of every man's good parts, a secret & villainous
contriver against me his natural brother ; therefore use
thy discretion—I had as lief thou didst break his neck
as his finger .

4　　　　　　　　　　　　And thou wert best look to't ; for if thou
dost him any slight disgrace, or if he do not mightily
grace himself on thee, he will practice against thee by
poison, entrap thee by some treacherous device, and never leave thee till he hath ta'en thy life by some indirect
means or other ; for I assure thee, (and almost with
tears I speak it) there is not one so young and so villainous this day living .

5　　　　　　　　　　　　I speak but brotherly of him,
but should I anatomize him to thee as he is, I must
blush, and weep, and thou must look pale and
wonder .

Oliver

1   Charles, I thanke thee for thy love to me, which
     thou shalt finde I will most kindly requite : I had my
     selfe notice of my Brothers purpose heerein, and have by
     under-hand meanes laboured to disswade him from it ;
     but he is resolute .

2   Ile tell thee Charles, it is the stubbor-
     nest yong fellow of France, full of ambition, an envious
     emulator of every mans good parts, a secret & villanous
     contriver against mee his naturall brother :therefore use
     thy discretion, I had as liefe thou didst breake his necke
     as his finger .

3   And thou wert best looke to't ; for if thou
     dost him any slight disgrace, or if hee doe not mightilie
     grace himselfe on thee, hee will practise against thee by
     poyson, entrap thee by some treacherous devise, and ne-
     ver leave thee till he hath tane thy life by some indirect
     meanes or other :for I assure thee, (and almost with
     teares I speake it) there is not one so young, and so vil-
     lanous this day living .

4   I speake but brotherly of him,
     but should I anathomize him to thee, as hee is, I must
     blush, and weepe, and thou must looke pale and
     wonder .

- from the opening emotional surround phrase

    " ; but he is resolute . "

    "full of ambition, an envious emulator of every mans good parts,"

    "therefore use thy discretion,"

    "entrap thee by some treacherous devise, and never leave thee till
    he hath tane thy life by some indirect…"

    "for I assure thee…there is not one so young, and so villanous this
    day living."

- while the few surround phrases underscore the seriousness of the
  danger, from the first ' ; but he is resolute .' through to

    " : therefore use thy discretion, I had as liefe thou didst breake his
    necke as his finger . / And thou wert best looke to't ; "

- as with the 'breake his necke' comment, Oliver's use of the long
  spelled words throughout seems to be released only at the appropriate times and designed for effect, often in short burst clusters—'un-
  der-hand meanes labour'd to disswade', 'mee his naturall brother',
  'teares I speake it'—as well as with the occasional single evocative
  word 'thanke', 'poyson', 'anathomize', and 'weepe'

- the only intellectual moment is probably the most telling of all, in
  the opening of F #2, the overall description of Orlando as a warning
  prelude of the dreadful things to come, 'Ile tell thee Charles, it is the
  stubbornest yong fellow of France', (2/0)

As You Like It

Orlando

Speake you so gently ? Pardon me I pray you,
2.7.106–119

Background: because of Adam's frail condition, Orlando has been forced to become what he claimed he never would be and is attempting force 'with a base and boistrous sword enforce/A theevish living on the common rode' by threatening to rob from Duke Senior and his men, demanding 'Forbeare, and eate no more'. Mercifully, perhaps through Orlando's 'enchanting' powers, the Duke has recognised his worth and talked him out of his criminal intent by freely offering him the food, suggesting 'Your gentlenesse shall force, more then your force/move us to gentlenesse.'. Hence Orlando's reply.

Style: one on one in front of a larger group

Where: Duke Senior's encampment in the forest of Arden

To Whom: Duke Senior, in front of his followers including Jaques and Amyens

# of Lines: 14

Probable Timing: 0.45 minutes

Orlando

1   Speak you so gently ?

2   Pardon me, I pray you .

3   I thought that all things had been savage here,
      And therefore put I on the countenance
      Of stern command'ment .

4   But what e'er you are
   That in this desert inaccessible,
   Under the shade of melancholy boughs,
   Loose, and neglect the creeping hours of time :
   If ever you have look'd on better days, ,
   If ever been where bells have knoll'd to church ,
   If ever sat at any good man's feast ,
   If ever from your eyelids wip'd a tear,
   And know what 'tis to pity, and be pitied,
   Let gentleness my strong enforcement be,
   In the which hope I blush, and hide my sword .

Orlando

1   Speake you so gently ?

2   Pardon me I pray you,
     I thought that all things had bin savage heere,
     And therefore put I on the countenance
     Of sterne command'ment .

3   But what ere you are
     That in this desert inaccessible,
     Under the shade of melancholly boughes,
     Loose, and neglect the creeping houres of time :
     If ever you have look'd on better dayes :
     If ever beene where bels have knoll'd to Church :
     If ever sate at any good mans feast :
     If ever from your eye-lids wip'd a teare,
     And know what 'tis to pittie, and be pittied :
     Let gentlenesse my strong enforcement be,
     In the which hope, I blush, and hide my Sword .

- the short emotional sentence opening the speech points to Orlando's surprise at the Duke's response to his threats (F #1, 0/1), while the explanation that he had only 'put on' (that is pretended) 'the countenance/Of sterne command'ment' is also restrainedly emotional (0/2 in the three lines of F #2), while, after an unembellished line and a half, the request for forgiveness becomes somewhat more emotionally released (2/10 in the last nine lines of the speech)

- Orlando's honesty and amazement at having been saved at the last minute from disgracing himself comes shining through in the few unembellished lines

    "Pardon me I pray you" &

    "But what ere you are/That in this desert inaccessible,"

- while the three successive surround phrases (the first three of six pure pentameter lines—somewhat unusual for this stage of Shakespeare's writings) clearly show the innate chivalric principles by which he would like to live

    " : If ever you have look'd on better dayes : / If ever beene where bels have knoll'd to Church : / If ever sate at any good mans feast :"

- though used to describe the situation of those who have found him and appeal for their forgiveness, the two clusters of long spellings might well underscore what he feels his own life has been to date, first that he has

    "Under the shade of melancholly boughes,/Loose and neglect the creeping houres of time : " (lines three and four of F #3, 0/4)

    "If ever from your eye-lids wiped a teare,/And know what 'tis to pittie, and be pittied : /Let gentlenesse my strong enforcement be" (lines seven to nine, F #3, 0/4)

As You Like It

Silvius

Oh Corin, that thou knew'st how I do love her.
between 2.3.25–43

Background: at his first on-stage appearance it's obvious that the shepherd Silvius has only thoughts for Phebe, the woman who 'scornes' him.

Style: as part of a two-handed scene in front of three hidden watchers

Where: unspecified, within the forest of Arden

To Whom: the older shepherd Corin, in front of the hidden Rosalind, Celia and Touchstone

# of Lines: 16

Probable Timing: 0.50 minutes

Take Note: After the explosive two-word opening 'Oh Corin', the speech is startling in that there is hardly any excess, as if Silvius is being extraordinarily quiet in trying to explain his deepest feelings (an unquiet sense of quiet perhaps) (2/4 in the first seventeen lines of the eighteen line speech).

Silvius

1   Oh Corin, that thou knew'st how I do love her !!

2   {But} , being old, thou canst not {†} ,
     Though in thy youth thou wast as true a lover
     As ever sigh'd upon a midnight pillow .

3   But if thy love were ever like to mine—
     As sure I think did never man love so—
     How many actions most ridiculous
     Hast thou been drawn to by thy fantasy ?

4   If thou rememb'rest not the slightest folly
     That ever love did make thee run into,
     Thou hast not lov'd ;
     Or if thou hast not sat as I do now,
     [Wearying] thy hearer in thy mistress praise,
     Thou hast not lov'd ;
     Or if thou hast not broke from company
     Abruptly, as my passion now makes me,
     Thou hast not lov'd .

5   O Phebe, Phebe, Phebe !

Silvius

1   Oh Corin, that thou knew'st how I do love her .

2   {But} , being old, thou canst not {†} ,
     Though in thy youth thou wast as true a lover
     As ever sigh'd upon a midnight pillow :
     But if thy love were ever like to mine,
     As sure I thinke did never man love so :
     How many actions most ridiculous,
     Hast thou beene drawne to by thy fantasie ?

3   If thou remembrest not the slightest folly,
     That ever love did make thee run into,
     Thou hast not lov'd .

4   Or if thou hast not sat as I doe now,
     [Wearing] thy hearer in thy Mistris praise,
     Thou hast not lov'd .

5   Or if thou hast not broke from companie,
     Abruptly as my passion now makes me,
     Thou hast not lov'd .

6   O Phebe, Phebe, Phebe .

- that this may be a fine example of irrational rationality can be seen in what most modern texts regard as F's peculiar sentence structure, for though calm in utterance, the F speech suggests great stress in putting the thoughts together

- Silvius opens with a short 'nothing-more-to-be-said' declaration of love (F1, 1/1)

- which is followed by an onrushed second sentence denying Corin's ability, though once 'as true a lover', to understand what he, Silvius, is going through (0/3 in the seven lines of F #2)

- and then come what most modern texts regard as three ungrammatical sentences, each itemising different degrees of his own 'ridiculous' actions—remembering 'the slightest folly'; wearying listeners with his 'Mistris praise'; breaking 'from companie/Abruptly'—as Silvius is about to do: and the fact that these are set as separate sentences allows for each to have a much greater separate impact, much more than that allowed by most modern texts which reset all three sentences into one generalised whole (mt. #4)

- and the final short sentence, common to both sets of texts, suddenly allows Phebe's name to be mentioned for the first time in the speech, which Silvius does with fervent repetition (3/0, F #6)

Twelfe Night, or, What you will
Duke

If Musicke be the food of Love, play on,
between 1.1.1–40

Background: this is one of Shakespeare's most famous opening speeches for character and play. If the actor keeps in mind that Orsino has been unsuccessfully wooing Olivia for quite some time, the speech is self-explanatory.

Style: general address to a small group

Where: somewhere in Orsino's palace

To Whom: an unspecified number of musicians and Lords, including Curio

# of Lines: 17

Probable Timing: 0.55 minutes

Take Note: That Orsino's thoughts, breath and utterances are highly affected throughout can be seen in the ten extra breath-thoughts scattered throughout the speech (marked ,), especially noticeable when romantic analogies are being made, as with the end of F #2 (the scent of music); F #5 ('fancie' alone being 'high fantasticall'); and the final F #6's excess (of lying 'sweet beds of Flowres'), two of which are heralded by the emotional semicolon, viz. F #2's final surround phrase '; Stealing, and giving Odour . ' and F #5's '; so full of shapes is fancie'.

Duke

1 If music be the food of love, play on,
Give me excess of it ; that surfeiting,
The appetite may sicken, and so die .

2 That strain again, it had a dying fall ;
O, it came o'er my ear like the sweet sound
That breaths upon a bank of violets,
Stealing and giving odor .

3   Enough, no more,
'Tis not so sweet now as it was before .

4 O spirit of love, how quick and fresh art thou,
That notwithstanding thy capacity
Receiveth as the sea , nought enters there,
Of what validity and pitch soe'er,
But falls into abatement and low price
Even in a minute .

5   So full of shapes is fancy,
That it alone is high fantastical .

---

6 Away before me to sweet beds of flow'rs,
Love-thoughts lie rich when canopied with bow'rs

Duke

1   If Musicke be the food of Love, play on,
     Give me excesse of it :that surfetting,
     The appetite may sicken, and so dye .

2   That straine agen, it had a dying fall :
     O, it came ore my eare, like the sweet sound
     That breathes upon a banke of Violets ;
     Stealing, and giving Odour .

3   Enough, no more,
     'Tis not so sweet now, as it was before .

4   O spirit of Love, how quicke and fresh art thou,
     That notwithstanding thy capacitie,
     Receiveth as the Sea .

5   Nought enters there,
     Of what validity, and pitch so ere,
     But falles into abatement, and low price
     Even in a minute ; so full of shapes is fancie,
     That it alone, is high fantasticall .

---

6   Away before me, to sweet beds of Flowres,
     Love-thoughts lye rich, when canopy'd with bowres .

- after the passionate and factual insistence of the opening line (2/1), the first two sentences are splendidly emotional (2/7 in the remaining six lines of F #1-2)

- Orsino's need for the 'food of Love' is heightened by the rest of the passage being set as surround phrases, save for the middle two lines of F #2

- however, the disillusionment of F #3's 'no more' is totally contrasting in its quiet unembellishment, and not just a melodramatic calm perhaps for thereafter, though some releases do re-establish themselves for the rest of the speech, and though they are more emotional than intellectual, they are nowhere near as many as before (3/6 in the last eleven lines including these unembellished ones, as opposed to 4/8 in seven lines of the opening)

- thus the brief intellectual recognition of F #4, the 'spirit of Love' receiving all worship 'as the Sea' should be paid great attention, perhaps as a sudden realisation by Orsino: and the final emotional last line flourish of 'Love-thoughts lye rich, when canopy'd with bowres.' sings out for the actor's and reader's attention and enjoyment

Twelfe Night, or, What you will

Sebastian

I perceive in you so excellent a touch
between 2.1.12–43

Background: at the top of the play, Sebastian believes he alone was saved from the ship-wreck and that his twin-sister Viola was drowned. Arriving in Illyria, having spent three months in the company of the man who saved him (Antonio), Sebastian (who for some reason has not yet revealed his true identity or life story) decides to strike out on his own, to Antonio's dismay, who wants to know at the very least where the young man is bound. Sebastian at last unburdens himself.

Style: as part of a two-handed scene

Where: unspecified, perhaps at the dock in Illyria

To Whom: his rescuer Antonio

# of Lines: 22

Probable Timing: 1.10 minutes

Take Note: F's onrush (five sentences as opposed to most modern texts' ten) shows that, almost throughout, Sebastian is not in full control of his feelings, initially presumably because at last he has to confess to have misrepresented himself for the last three months, and then, as F's orthography shows, the memory of his (supposedly) dead sister adds even more to his inability to handle himself as tidily as most modern texts would have the actor believe.

Sebastian

1   {⸸} I perceive in you so excellent a touch
of modesty, that you will not extort from me what I am
willing to keep in ; therefore it charges me in manners
the rather to express myself .

2   You must know of me
then, Antonio, my name is Sebastian, which I call'd Rodo-
rigo; my father was that Sebastian of Messaline, whom I
know you have heard of .

3   He left behind him myself
and a sister, both born in an hour .

4   If the heavens had
been pleas'd, would we had so ended .

5   But you, sir, alter'd that, for some hour before you took me from the
breach of the sea was my sister drown'd .

---

6   A lady, sir, though it was said she much resem-
bled me, was yet of many accounted beautiful ; but though
I could not with such estimable wonder over far believe that, yet thus far I will boldly publish her : she
bore a mind that envy could not but call fair .

7   She is
drown'd already, sir, with salt water, though I seem to
drown her remembrance again with more .

---

8   Fare
ye well at once ; my bosom is full of kindness, and I
am yet so near the manners of my mother, that upon the
least occasion more mine eyes will tell tales of me .

9   I am
bound to the Count Orsino's Court .

10   Farewell .

Sebastian

1　　　　　　　　{†} I perceive in you so excellent a touch
of modestie, that you will not extort from me, what I am
willing to keepe in : therefore it charges me in manners,
the rather to expresse my selfe : you must know of mee
then Antonio, my name is Sebastian(which I call'd Rodo-
rigo) my father was that Sebastian of Messaline, whom I
know you have heard of .

2　　　　　　　　　　　　He left behinde him, my selfe,
and a sister, both borne in an houre : if the Heavens had
beene pleas'd, would we had so ended .

3　　　　　　　　　　　　　　　But you sir, al-
ter'd that, for some houre before you tooke me from the
breach of the sea, was my sister drown'd .

4　A Lady sir, though it was said shee much resem-
bled me, was yet of many accounted beautiful :but thogh
I could not with such estimable wonder over-farre be-
leeve that, yet thus farre I will boldly publish her, shee
bore a mind that envy could not but call faire : Shee is
drown'd already sir with salt water, though I seeme to
drowne her remembrance againe with more .

5　　　　　　　　　　　　　　　Fare
ye well at once, my bosome is full of kindnesse, and I
am yet so neere the manners of my mother, that upon the
least occasion more, mine eyes will tell tales of me : I am
bound to the Count Orsino's Court, farewell .

- the opening starts very carefully, the first two unembellished phrases leading to the surround phrase which sums the essential chivalric honor by which he (seems to wish to) conducts himself
    " : therefore it charges me in manners, the rather to expresse my selfe : "
and then the information that he wishes Antonio to have is handled as factually as possible (5/1, the last three lines of F #1)

- the facts of his sister's death are seemingly emotionally burned in his brain, as the surround phrases of F #2 (1/4) show
    " . He left behind him, my selfe, and a sister, both borne in an houre : if the Heavens had beene pleas'd, would we had so ended . "

- the recollection that he rather than his sister has been saved is, naturally, emotional (0/2, F #3), and though it seems that he tries to contain himself as he describes her to Anthonio (1/1, the first two lines of F #4), as he recalls the beauty of her mind, joining this via the fast-link ungrammatical colon (the last in F #4) to her drowning (the drowning set as a separate sentence by most modern texts), the emotional floodgates open (1/8, in the remaining five lines of the onrushed F #4)

- the attempted farewell stays emotional (0/3, the first three lines of F #5), and it seems very clear that his claim to be close to tears is very genuine, as the (rare in this speech) unembellished line
    "that upon the least occasion more, mine eyes will tell tales of me"
will testify

- the final doubly ungrammatical moment of the facts as to where he is going (3/0, the last line of the speech), his final word of 'farewell', plus the claim of trying to avoid tears being tacked together as one sentence (via first a fast link colon, and then a fastlink comma) suggests that Sebastian has still not managed to regain self-control—unlike his modern counterpart who is given two separate sentences (mt. #9-10) to make a more tidy departure

Twelfe Night, or, What you will

Sebastian

This is the ayre, that is the glorious Sunne,
4.3. 1–21

Background: mistaken by Olivia for Cesario, the public male perso-na disguise of his twin sister Viola, Sebastian has been vigorously wooed by Olivia and fallen under her spell. This is his first time alone since her all out sensual love-driven onslaught.

Style: solo

Where: somewhere in house or gardens

To Whom: self and direct audience address

# of Lines: 21

Probable Timing: 1.10 minutes

Take Note: Though the first sentences match, according to F's on-rushed second sentence Sebastian's apparent self-control quickly disappears once the troubling thoughts of possible insanity get in the way of his opening reverie, especially since he cannot seek Antonio's advice.

Sebastian

1   This is the air, that is the glorious sun,
     This pearl she gave me, I do feel't and see't,
     And though 'tis wonder that enwraps me thus,
     Yet 'tis not madness .

2   Where's Antonio then ?

3   I could not find him at the Elephant,
     Yet there he was, and there I found this credit,
     That he did range the town to seek me out .

4   His counsel now might do me golden service,
     For though my soul disputes well with my sense,
     That this may be some error, but no madness,
     Yet doth this accident and flood of fortune
     So far exceed all instance, all discourse,
     That I am ready to distrust mine eyes,
     And wrangle with my reason that persuades me
     To any other trust but that I am mad,
     Or else the lady's mad ; yet if 'twere so,
     She could not sway her house, command her followers,
     Take, and give back affairs, and their dispatch,
     With such a smooth, discreet, and stable bearing
     As I perceive she do's .

5   There's something in't
     That is deceivable .

6   But here the lady comes .

Sebastian

1   This is the ayre, that is the glorious Sunne,
This pearle she gave me, I do feel't, and see't,
And though tis wonder that enwraps me thus,
Yet 'tis not madnesse .

2   Where's Anthonio then,
I could not finde him at the Elephant,
Yet there he was, and there I found this credite,
That he did range the towne to seeke me out,
His councell now might do me golden service,
For though my soule disputes well with my sence,
That this may be some error, but no madnesse,
Yet doth this accident and flood of Fortune,
So farre exceed all instance, all discourse,
That I am readie to distrust mine eyes,
And wrangle with my reason that perswades me
To any other trust, but that I am mad,
Or else the Ladies mad ; yet if 'twere so,
She could not sway her house, command her followers,
Take, and give backe affayres, and their dispatch,
With such a smooth, discreet, and stable bearing
As I perceive she do's : there's something in't
That is deceiveable .

3   But heere the Lady comes .

- the tug of opposites of mad versus not mad are often expressed by very quiet unembellished lines, as if Sebastian must restrain himself lest the dream disappear altogether: thus the 'not mad' sequences include, first about the ring

    "I do feel't, and see't"

  and the denial of Olivia's 'madnesse' for

    " ; yet if 'twere so,/She could not sway her house, command her followers,/ ... /With such a smooth, discreet, and stable bearing/ As I perceive she do's"

  while, the unembellished possibly mad sequences include

    " . . this may be some error,/ ... /Yet doth this accident... /...exceed all instance, all discourse,/That I am readie to distrust mine eyes,/And wrangle with my reason... /...but that I am mad,"

- the only surround phrase wonderfully sums up the whole problem

    " : there's something in't/That is deceiveable . "

  thus matching Viola and Olivia who earlier also believed they could not solve their dilemmas (speeches #7 and #9 above, respectively)

- thus the speech opens full of (joyful?) emotion (1/4, F #1)

- the inability to locate Antonio is at first handled passionately (2/2, the first two lines of F #2), then quickly turns to emotion as Sebastian realises how much he needs Antonio's advice (0/6, the next five lines)

- as a result of all the unembellished phrases discussed above, the possibility of madness in either himself or Olivia 'yet doth this accident...' is handled very gingerly (an occasional factual release, 2/1 the first five and a half lines to the semicolon), and then his losing himself in how Olivia conducts herself becomes slightly emotional (0/3 the remaining five lines of F #2), which turns to passion (1/1 in the very short F #3) as she joins him on-stage

Alls Well that Ends Well

Parrolles

Are you meditating on virginitie ?
between 1.1.110–138

Background: Hellen's recently deceased father, a physician of great renown, was doctor to the house of Rossillion, where he and Hellen lived. Hellen has fallen in love with Bertram who has just become the head of the family, and thus the Count, following the death of his father, a long-time friend of the King. In her eyes, marriage with Bertram would be totally impossible because of the differences in their social standing, and also because he is totally unaware of her feelings. Bertram is about to leave Rossillion for the French Court in Paris, guided by Lafew (an elderly friend of his father's and the king's) and accompanied by Parrolles (a blow-hard 'miles gloriosus'). Unaware that Hellen knows him for what he is ('a notorious Liar', 'great way foole', and 'solie a coward'), Parrolles tries his wit (and luck?) with her in a very risqué conversation.

Style: part of a two handed scene

Where: somewhere in the house or grounds of Rossillion

To Whom: Hellen

# of Lines: 17

Probable Timing: 0.55 minutes

Parrolles

1   Are you meditating on virginity? {†}

2   Man is enemy to Virginity; {†}
    and {your} virginity though valiant, in the defense
    yet is weak {†}

3   Man, setting down before you, will
    undermine you and blow you up .{†}

4   There {is} no military policy how vir-
    gins might blow up men {.}

5   {Yet} virginity being blown down, man will
    quicklier be blown up {†}

6   It is not politic in the commonwealth of
    nature to preserve virginity .

7   Loss of virginity, is
    rational increase, and there was never virgin [got] till
    virginity was first lost .

8   That you were made of is met-
    tall to make virgins .

9   Virginity, by being once lost,
    may be ten times found ; by being ever kept, it is ever
    lost .
        'Tis too cold a companion ; away with't !

----

10   'Tis against the
    rule of nature .

11   To speak on the part of virginity is
    to accuse your mothers, which is most infallible diso-
    bedience .

Parrolles

1   Are you meditating on virginitie ? {†}

2   Man is enemie to virginitie, {†} and {your} virginitie though valiant, in the defence yet is weak {†}

3   Man setting downe before you, will undermine you, and blow you up .{†}

4   There {is} no Military policy how Virgins might blow up men {.}

5   {Yet} Virginity beeing blowne downe, Man will quicklier be blowne up {†}

6   It is not politicke, in the Common-wealth of Nature, to preserve virginity .

7   Losse of Virginitie, is rationall encrease, and there was never Virgin[goe], till virginitie was first lost .

8   That you were made of, is mettall to make Virgins .

9   Virginitie, by beeing once lost, may be ten times found :by being ever kept, it is ever lost : 'tis too cold a companion :Away with't .

---

10   'Tis against the rule of Nature .

11   To speake on the part of virginitie, is to accuse your Mothers :which is most infallible disobedience .

- the speech starts very carefully with two unembellished sentences when even the topic, 'virginitie', is presented in its short spelling form—either a sound seduction tactic or, admittedly less likely, a sign of a man not too sure of how to begin

- the first off-colour image, of a man 'setting downe before you', is the first time emotion makes an appearance (F #3, 0/1), with the possibility that Parrolles is not quite as in control as he would wish to be evidenced by the first extra breath-thought that appears (marked ,), as if he needs to control himself before offering the rather graphic monosyllabic/unembellished image 'and blow you up.'

- for the next off-colour sequence, though the suggestion that women cannot 'blow up men' starts intellectually (2/0, F #4), the follow through is much more passionately emotional (2/4, F #5)

- as F #6's argument not to 'preserve virginity' is advanced, while it and the following general chop-logic suggestion that loss of (now capitalised) 'Virginitie' will only serve to breed more virgins (F #7-8) stays passionate (5/6), it seems that Parrolles might be somewhat excited by his own logic, for three more extra breath-thoughts suddenly appear in F #6 and #8

- then, for some reason it seems that Parrolles feels he needs to change his approach, for though the images remain essentially the same, F #9's build to his blatant urging of Hellen ' : Away with it . ' is completely made up of four surround phrases

  " . Virginitie, by beeing once lost, may be ten times found : by being
     ever kept, it is ever lost : 'tis too cold a companion : Away with't ."
  the second and third unembellished, as if to speak any louder might break the mood

- Parrolles' F #10 attempt to sum up, though seemingly relaxed (1/0), is via a very short sentence, suggesting that in his desire to seduce, no more can be said, yet obviously there must be, for the F #11 'Mothers' argument (unnecessary if he had been successful) is again composed of surround lines, starting with passion (1/1), and ending in an (enforced?) unembellished calm which may belie what is going on underneath

Alls Well that Ends Well

Parrolles

Virginitie breedes mites, much like a Cheese,
between 1.1.141–164

Background: While Parolles prior speech opened the conversation in general, in this speech Parolles attempts to press his point home.

Style: both, as part of a two handed scene

Where: somewhere in the house or grounds of Rossillion

To Whom: Hellen

# of Lines: 18

Probable Timing: 0.55 minutes

Take Note: Whereas in the first speech intellect and emotion virtually matched (12/10), in this follow-up emotions are given much more sway (11/26 overall), perhaps another sign that Parrolles' seduction efforts are not proceeding according to plan.

Parrolles

1 Virginity breeds mites, much like a
cheese, consumes itself to the very paring, and so
dies with feeding his own stomach .

2   Besides, virginity is peevish, proud, idle, made of self-love, which
is the most inhibited sin in the canon .

3   Keep it not,
you cannot choose but lose by't .

4   Out with't !

5   Within
[t'one] year it will make itself two, which is a goodly in-
crease, and the principal itself not much the worse .

6 Away with't !

---

7 The longer kept, the less worth .

8   Off with't while 'tis
vendible ; answer the time of request .

9   Virginity, like
an old courtier, wears her cap out of fashion, richly
suited, but unsuitable—just like the brooch & the tooth-
pick, which [wear] not now .

10   Your date is better in your
pie and your porridge [than] in your cheek ; and your
virginity, your old virginity, is like one of our French
wither'd pears, it looks ill, it eats drily, marry 'tis a
wither'd pear ; it was formerly better, marry yet 'tis a
wither'd pear .

11   Will you any thing with it ?

Parrolles

1   Virginitie breedes mites, much like a
Cheese, consumes it selfe to the very payring, and so
dies with feeding his owne stomacke .

2   Besides, Virginitie is peevish, proud, ydle, made of selfe-love, which
is the most inhibited sinne in the Cannon .

3   Keepe it not,
you cannot choose but loose by't .

4   Out with't : within
[ten] yeare it will make it selfe two, which is a goodly in-
crease, and the principall it selfe not much the worse .

5   Away with't .

_____

6   The longer kept, the lesse worth : Off with't while 'tis
vendible .

7   Answer the time of request, Virginitie like
an olde Courtier, weares her cap out of fashion, richly
suted, but unsuteable, just like the brooch & the tooth-
pick, which [were] not now : your Date is better in your
Pye and your Porredge, [then] in your cheeke : and your
virginity, your old virginity, is like one of our French
wither'd peares, it lookes ill, it eates drily, marry 'tis a
wither'd peare : it was formerly better, marry yet 'tis a
wither'd peare : Will you any thing with it ?

- the return to chop-logic, arguing kept virginity consumes itself, is highly emotional (1/5, F #1)

- and F #2's moral attack on the concept of virginity (as being 'peevish, proud, ydle, made of selfe-love') and F #3's repeated-from-the-first-speech-urging to 'Keepe it not' continue the emotional drive (2/7, F #2-3)

- it seems that Hellen gives him neither response nor encouragement, for this is immediately followed up by yet another change in style, a very short monosyllabic unembellished surround phrase opening F #4 '. Out with't : '—again an attempt at a confidential invitation perhaps

- that this doesn't work or is not deemed enough can be seen in that Parrolles then switches to pure emotion once more (F #4, 0/4) to argue yet again lose-your-virginity-now-so-as-to-make-more, which had little or no effect in speech #1

- and once more the F #5 urging 'Away with't.', though seemingly calm, is offered via a very short unembellished sentence, as if the appearance of calm was all that was needed to succeed

- however, what ensues is certainly not calm, for the 'longer kept, the lesse worth' argument is made via a passionate short two surround-phrase sentence (F #6, 1/1), and the suggestion/demand/bleat 'Answer the time of request' that opens F #7 becomes passionate (2/3 in the first three and a half lines)

- and the passion intensifies in the age-is-better-elsewhere argument, (3/3 in the one colon—implying logic rather than emotion—created surround line ' :your Date is better in your Pye and your Porredge, [then] in your cheeke :)

- and the whole finishes (desperately? humourously?) emotionally (2/5, the end of the argument formulated once more by two surround phrases of somewhat less than salubrious imagery ' : it was formerly better, marry yet 'tis a wither'd peare : Will you any thing with it ? .'

The Winter's Tale

Clowne

I have seene two such sights, by Sea & by Land :
between 3.3.80–103

Background: as with his father the first speech for the character also known as the Young Shepheard is virtually self-explanatory. The ship wrecked is the one that brought Antigonus and Hermione's about-to-be-abandoned baby-daughter to Bohemia, the 'poore Gentleman' torn apart by the bear is, as the Clowne explains, Antigonus.

Style: as part of a two-handed scene

Where: somewhere on the shores of Bohemia

To Whom: his father, the Old Shepherd

# of Lines: 19

Probable Timing: 1.00 minutes

Clown

1   I have seen two such sights, by sea & by land !

2   But I am not to say it is a sea, for it is now the sky, be-
twixt the firmament and it you cannot thrust a bodkin's
point .

---

3   I would you did but see how it chafes, how it ra-
ges, how it takes up the shore !

4   But that's not to the point .

5   O, the most piteous cry of the poor souls !

6   Sometimes
to see 'em, and not to see 'em ; now the ship boring
the moon with her mainmast, and anon swallow'd
with yest and froth, as you'ld thrust a cork into a hogs
head .

7   And then for the land-service, to see how the
bear tore out his shoulder-bone, how he cried to me
for help, and said his name was Antigonus, a nobleman .

8   But to make an end of the ship, to see how the sea flap-
dragon'd it ; but, first, how the poor souls roar'd, and,
the sea mock'd them ; and how the poor gentleman
roar'd, and the bear mock'd him, both roaring louder
[than] the sea or weather .

---

9 {‡}   I have not wink'd since I saw these
sights .

10   The men are not yet cold under water, nor the
bear half din'd on the gentleman .

11   He's at it now .

Clowne

1   I have seene two such sights, by Sea & by Land :
but I am not to say it is a Sea, for it is now the skie, be-
twixt the Firmament and it, you cannot thrust a bodkins
point .

---

2   I would you did but see how it chafes, how it ra-
ges, how it takes up the shore, but that's not to the point :
Oh, the most pitteous cry of the poore soules, sometimes
to see 'em, and not to see 'em : Now the Shippe boaring
the Moone with her maine Mast, and anon swallowed
with yest and froth, as you'ld thrust a Corke into a hogs-
head .

3   And then for the Land-service, to see how the
Beare tore out his shoulder-bone, how he cride to mee
for helpe, and said his name was Antigonus, a Nobleman :
But to make an end of the Ship, to see how the Sea flap-
dragon'd it : but first, how the poore soules roared, and,
the sea mock'd them : and how the poore Gentleman
roared, and the Beare mock'd him, both roaring lowder
[then] the sea, or weather .

---

4 {†}   I have not wink'd since I saw these
sights : the men are not yet cold under water, nor the
Beare halfe din'd on the Gentleman : he's at it now .

- unlike his father, the Clowne's few surround phrases are not a character style, but highlight the most painful of the sights he has just seen, from the opening
     " . I have seene two such sights, by Sea & Land ; "
  with the sounds as equally disturbing as what he saw
    " : Oh, the most pitteous cry of the poore soules, sometimes
     to see 'em, and not see 'em : "
  as the emotional opening (1/4, the first two phrases), and sudden unembellished quiet of the last two show, echoed later by the recollection
     " : but first how the poore soules roared, and, the sea mock'd them : "
  and the speech ends with the details seemingly burned in his brain, as all three surround phrases that make up the final F #4 show

- the speech starts intellectually (4/1, F #1)

- then, fascinatingly, his first recollection of the storm being so violent that he cannot distinguish between the sea and the sky
     "you cannot thrust a bodkins point .I would you did but see how
      it chafes, how it rages, how it takes up the shore, but that's not
      to the point:"
  is completely unembellished; perhaps even he is surprised by it's ferocity

- and while the 'Oh, the most pitteous cry of the poore soules' is remembered emotionally (1/4), his visual memory of what he saw at sea turns passionate (5/5 in F #2's last two and half lines), as is the memory of Antigonus and the bear (4/4, the first three lines of F #3)

- then, as one thought piles on top of the other, so the accompanying styles change too, returning to the idea of the ship is intellectual (3/0); the sound of the 'poore soules' emotional once more (0/2); and the 'poore Gentleman' both (2/3)—a lovely tug of war for the actor to explore

- the effect on him seems profound, for the start of F #4 'I have not wink'd since I saw these sights : the men are not yet cold under water' forces him into unembellished quiet once more, though the action of the 'Beare' still seems disturbing (2/2 in just eight words)

The Winter's Tale

Florizell

Thou deer'st Perdita,
between 4.4.40–54

Background: by accident Florizell, son to Polixenes, King of Bohemia, met Perdita, a young woman reared from birth as daughter to the old Shepheard , in reality the abandoned daughter of Hermione and Leontes) and they have fallen in love. To prevent parental interference based on class distinctions, they have hidden their love from his father, and pretended to those who have reared her that he is merely a land-owner with a 'worthy-feeding's named Doricles. This is Florizell's response to Perdita's fear that his father will find out all and end their relationship.

Style: as part of a two-handed scene, with a larger group on-stage, not attempting to listen

Where: Bohemia, outdoors, where the sheep-shearing festival is to be held

To Whom: Perdita, in front of a larger group finishing preparations for the sheep-shearing festival

# of Lines: 15

Probable Timing: 0.50 minutes

Take Note: Florizell's attempt to assuage Perdita's fears start out determinedly intellectual (6/3, F #1), the first of only two surround phrases in the speech ' : Or Ile be thine (my Faire)/Or not my Fathers . ' making it as plain as he possibly can how devoted he is.

Florizell

1   Thou dear'st Perdita,
    With these forc'd thoughts I prithee darken not
    The mirth o'th'feast .

2   Or I'll be thine, my fair,
    Or not my father's ; for I cannot be
    Mine own, nor any thing to any, if
    I be not thine .

3   To this I am most constant,
    Though destiny say no .

4   Be merry, gentle!
    Strangle such thoughts as these with any thing
    That you behold the while .

5   Your guests are coming :
    Lift up your countenance, as it were the day
    Of celebration of that nuptial, which
    We two have sworn shall come .

---

6   See, your guests approach,
    Address yourself to entertain them sprightly,
    And let's be red with mirth .

Florizell

1 Thou deer'st Perdita,
   With these forc'd thoughts, I prethee darken not
   The Mirth o'th'Feast : Or Ile be thine(my Faire)
   Or not my Fathers .

2   For I cannot be
   Mine owne, nor any thing to any, if
   I be not thine .

3   To this I am most constant,
   Though destiny say no .

4   Be merry (Gentle)
   Strangle such thoughts as these, with any thing
   That you behold the while .

5   Your guests are comming :
   Lift up your countenance, as it were the day
   Of celebration of that nuptiall, which
   We two have sworne shall come .

---

6 See, your Guests approach,
   Addresse your selfe to entertaine them sprightly,
   And let's be red with mirth .

- and it looks as if this hard-working reassurance may quietly take effect, for there are very few further releases within the speech, and those there are, are essentially emotional (2/6 in the final ten lines, as compared to 6/2 in the first three)

- thus the next three sentences of reassurance as to his being nothing 'if/I be not thine', unequivocally stating 'To this I am most constant' and that she should thus 'Strangle' the negative thoughts she is currently bedeviled by, are almost completely unembellished (1/1 in the five lines F #2-4), his calm hopefully calming her down

- and while his reminder that she must 'entertaine' the 'Guests' who 'are comming' for the sheep-shearing (of which, as her father later describes her, she is the presiding ceremonial 'Hostesse of the meeting') is emotional (1/6, F #5-6) there are still some very gentle unembellished personal comments, as

  "Lift up your countenance, as it were the day/Of celebration…"

of their eventual wedding, and the charming suggestion that if she is 'red' (i.e. blushing—presumably at the thought of their 'nuptiall') then it might be better that

  "And let's be red with mirth."

The Winter's Tale

Autolicus

Ha, ha, what a Foole Honestie is ? and Trust (his
4.4.595–618

Background: following Polixines' public explosion at Florizell, Perdita, and the Old Shepheard (speech #15 above) and subsequent abrupt finish to the festival, Autolicus, a charmingly seductive, itinerant peddler and expert pick-pocket, shares a moment's summation of his achievements on this very profitable (for him) day.

Style: solo

Where: Bohemia, outdoors, where the sheep-shearing festival is breaking up

To Whom: direct audience address

# of Lines: 23

Probable Timing: 1.10 minutes

Autolicus

1   Ha, ha, what a fool Honesty is ! and Trust, his
    sworn brother, a very simple gentleman !

2   I have sold
    all my trumpery; not a counterfeit stone, not a ribbon,
    glass, pomander, brooch, table-book, ballad, knife,
    tape, glove, shoe-tie, bracelet, horn-ring, to keep
    my pack from fasting .

3   They throng who should buy first,
    as if my trinkets had been hallow'd and brought a be-
    nediction to the buyer ; by which means I saw whose
    purse was best in picture, and what I saw, to my good
    use I rememb'red .

4   My clown (who wants but some-
    thing to be a reasonable man) grew so in love with the
    wenches' song, that he would not stir his pettitoes,
    till he had both tune and words, which so drew the rest
    of the herd to me that all their other senses stuck in
    ears .

5   You might have pinch'd a placket, it was sense-
    less ; 'twas nothing to geld a codpiece of a purse ; I
    would have filed keys of that hung in chains.

6   No
    hearing, no feeling, but my sir's song, and admiring the
    nothing of it .

7   So that in this time of lethargy I pick'd
    and cut most of their festival purses ; and had not the
    old man come in with a whoobub against his daugh-
    ter, and the King's son, and scar'd my choughs from
    the chaff, I had not left a purse alive in the whole
    army .

Autolicus

1   Ha, ha, what a Foole Honestie is ? and Trust(his
     sworne brother) a very simple Gentleman .

2   I have sold
     all my Tromperie : not a counterfeit Stone, not a Ribbon,
     Glasse, Pomander, Browch, Table-booke, Ballad, Knife,
     Tape, Glove, Shooe-tye, Bracelet, Horne-Ring, to keepe
     my Pack from fasting : they throng who should buy first,
     as if my Trinkets had beene hallowed, and brought a be-
     nediction to the buyer : by which meanes, I saw whose
     Purse was best in Picture ; and what I saw, to my good
     use, I remembred .

3   My Clowne (who wants but some-
     thing to be a reasonable man) grew so in love with the
     Wenches Song, that hee would not stirre his Petty-toes,
     till he had both Tune and Words, which so drew the rest
     of the Heard to me, that all their other Sences stucke in
     Eares : you might have pinch'd a Placket, it was sence-
     lesse ; 'twas nothing to gueld a Cod-peece of a Purse : I
     would have fill'd Keyes of that hung in Chaynes : no
     hearing, no feeling, but my Sirs Song, and admiring the
     Nothing of it .

4   So that in this time of Lethargie, I pickd
     and cut most of their Festivall Purses : And had not the
     old-man come in with a Whoo-bub against his Daugh-
     ter, and the Kings Sonne, and scar'd my Chowghes from
     the Chaffe, I had not left a Purse alive in the whole
     Army .

- Autolicus is rarely at rest, thus the two small unembellished moments, the first heightened by being an emotional () surround phrase

    " ; and what I saw, to my good use, I remembred . "

  followed almost straightway by the less than flattering description of the young Clowne (the Old Shepheard's son)

    " (who wants but something to be a reasonable man)"

  should be relished as moments when Autolicus is at his most confidentially quiet

- the pinnacle of his success seems to be underscored by the successive surround phrases, heralded first with F #1's start

    " . Ha, ha, what a Foole Honestie is ? and Trust (his sworne brother) a very simple Gentleman . "

- followed by F #2's

    " : by which meanes, I saw whose Purse was best in Picture ; and what I saw, to my good use, I remembred . "

  in turn followed by the end of F #3/beginning of F #4

    " : you might have pinch'd a Placket, it was sencelesse ; 'twas

  nothing to gueld a Cod-peece of a Purse : I would have fill'd Keyes of that hung in Chaynes : no hearing, no feeling, but my Sirs Song, and admiring the Nothing of it . So that in this time of Lethargie, I pickd and cut most of their Festivall Purses :"

- overall the speech is highly factual/intellectual (51/26 in twenty-three—presumably celebratory—lines), with many of the emotional releases coming in small clusters, as with the description of what he has sold, 'Glasse,…, Browch, Table-booke,…, Shooe-tye,…, Horne-Ring'; the foolishness of prospective purchasers enticed by the Clowne's reaction to Autolicus' singing which drew the others, described as 'the Heard to me, that all their Sences stucke in Eares'; the joy of filching, as 'gueld a Cod-peece of a Purse : I would have fill'd Keyes of that hung in Chaynes'; and the final 'Whoo-bub' about Perdita and Florizell which 'scar'd my Chowghes from the Chaffe'

The Winter's Tale

Clowne

You are well met (Sir :) you deny'd to fight
between 5.2.128–145

Background: far from the awful doom prophesied by Autolicus for the Old Shepherd and the Clowne, once Leontes learned from the documents produced by the Old Shepherd that Perdita was Leontes' own daughter, he promptly granted the Old Shepherd and the Clowne the rank of Gentlemen, and provided them clothing and status accordingly, as the Clowne is only to eager to point out.

Style: as part of a three-handed scene

Where: somewhere in the palace of Sicilia

To Whom: Autolicus, in front of the Old Shepherd

# of Lines: 14

Probable Timing: 0.45 minutes

Take Note: With his new promotion to the rank of gentleman the Clowne shows virtually no self-control, either in vocal release (24/18), or in surround phrases (at least ten) in just thirteen lines overall.

Clown

1   You are well met, sir .

2   You denied to fight
with me this other day, because I was no gentleman
born .

3   See you these clothes ?

4   Say you see them not
and think me still no gentleman borne .

5   You were best
say these robes are not gentlemen born .

6   Give me the
lie, do ; and try whether I am not now a gentleman
born .

---

7   {For I} have been so any time these four hours.

---

8 {†}   {And} I was a gentleman born before my father ; for the King's son took me by the
hand, and call'd me brother ; and then the two kings
call'd my father brother ; and then the Prince, my brother, and the Princess, my sister, call'd my father, father;
and so we wept ; and there was the first gentleman like
tears that ever we shed .

Clowne

1   You are well met(Sir :) you deny'd to fight
with mee this other day, because I was no Gentleman
borne .

2   See you these Clothes ? say you see them not,
and thinke me still no Gentleman borne : You were best
say these Robes are not Gentlemen borne .

3   Give me the
Lye : doe : and try whether I am not now a Gentleman
borne .

---

4   {For I} have been so any time these foure houres .

---

5 {†}   {And} I was a Gentleman borne before my Father : for the Kings Sonne tooke me by the
hand, and call'd mee Brother : and then the two Kings
call'd my Father Brother : and then the Prince(my Brother) and the Princesse(my Sister) call'd my Father, Father;
and so wee wept : and there was the first Gentleman-like
teares that ever we shed .

- the Clowne's excitement is almost tangible, both with the opening surround phrase monosyllabic challenge, and the passion that fills the first four lines (4/5)

- then, as with so many foolish Shakespeare characters, the next stage of his proof that he is a 'Gentleman' becomes based on his outward appearance, a somewhat intellectual attachment to his clothing (2/1, the last line of F #2) is pushed even harder, with passion (2/3) and three surround phrases completely forming F #3

- the sweet if foolish brag that he has been a gentleman 'these foure houres' is pushed emotionally (0/2), the shortness of F #4 perhaps suggesting that he is still somewhat stunned by the whole idea

- and then the recalling of the joyous events that took place with both Kings swamps him completely, starting with the passionate description of how the 'Kings Sonne…call'd mee Brother' (5/4, the first two lines of F #5), and the vastly intellectual releases of the new inter-family naming of names (9/1, the next two and half lines)

- while the final recollection of 'so wee wept' becomes almost too much to bear, for not only is it emotional (1/2), the recollection is formed by two surround phrases, the first heightened by the only emotional in the speech

The Tempest
Caliban

All the infections that the Sunne suckes up
2.2.1–17

Background: now gathering the wood as Prospero charged, and alone, Caliban gives vent to his feelings, presumably in part trying to win the audience to his side.

Style: solo

Where: somewhere uninhabited on the island, possibly near the shore

To Whom: direct audience address

# of Lines: 17

Probable Timing: 0.55 minutes

Take Note: Even though the first sentences match, thereafter F's single onrushed sentence shows a far more disturbed character than do the five sentences most modern texts split it into: and F's orthography shows an interesting pattern in that after the opening passionate explosion (6/6), despite the onrushed F #2, Caliban begins to calm down and establish some form of self control.

Caliban

1 All the infections that the sun sucks up
   From bogs, fens, flats, on Prosper fall, and make him
   By inch-meal a disease !

2   His spirits hear me,
   And yet I needs must curse .

3   But they'll nor pinch,
   Fright me with urchin-shows, pitch me i'th mire,
   Nor lead me, like a firebrand, in the dark
   Out of my way, unless he bid'em; but
   For every trifle are they set upon me,
   Sometime like apes that mow and chatter at me,
   And after bite me ; then like hedge hogs which
   Lie tumbling in my barefoot way, and mount
   Their pricks at my footfall ; sometime am I
   All wound with adders, who with cloven tongues
   Do hiss me into madness .
                    [Enter Trinculo]

4   Lo, now lo,
   Here comes a spirit of his, and to torment me
   For bringing wood in slowly .

5   I'll fall flat,
   Perchance he will not mind me .

Caliban

1   All the infections that the Sunne suckes up
From Bogs, Fens, Flats, on Prosper fall, and make him
By ynch-meale a disease : his Spirits heare me,
And yet I needes must curse .

2   But they'll nor pinch,
Fright me with Urchyn-shewes, pitch me i'th mire,
Nor lead me like a fire-brand, in the darke
Out of my way, unlesse he bid'em; but
For every trifle, are they set upon me,
Sometime like Apes, that moe and chatter at me,
And after bite me : then like Hedg-hogs, which
Lye tumbling in my bare-foote way, and mount
Their pricks at my foot-fall : sometime am I
All wound with Adders, who with cloven tongues
Doe hisse me into madnesse :
        [**Enter Trinculo**]
                    Lo, now Lo,
Here comes a Spirit of his, and to torment me
For bringing wood in slowly : I'le fall flat,
Perchance he will not minde me .

- that Caliban can never be in full control is summed up in the surround phrase that ends F #1, ': his Spirits heare me,/And yet I needes must curse. .', while the somewhat longer surround phrases that end the speech sum up both his fears and his response to danger

    " : then like Hedg-hogs, which/Lye tumbling in my bare-foote way, and mount/Their pricks at my foot-fall : sometime am I/All wound with Adders, who with cloven tongues/Doe hisse me into madnesse : Lo, now Lo,/Here comes a Spirit of his, and to torment me /For bringing wood in slowly : I'le fall flat,/ Perchance he will not minde me ."

- Caliban seems to want to present himself as a calm character, only to have this mask suddenly destroyed by bursts of release as with the emotional 'Sunne suckes up' and the intellectual 'Bogs, Fens, Flats, on Prosper fall' all in the first sentence; or the emotional 'Doe hisse me into madnesse' and the intellectual ' ; Lo, now Lo,/here comes a Spirit of his,' in the second sentence

- the explosion of the first sentence (6/6 in just three and a half lines) becomes more controlled, that is, proportionately less releases (just 4/9 in F #2's first ten lines) but nevertheless emotional rather than intellectual in describing what Prospero's 'Spirits' do to him—an attempt at gaining the audience's empathy/sympathy perhaps?

- the (mistaken) realisation that Prospero has sent another 'Spirit' to torment him (in fact the character entering is the very human Trinculo, jester to Alonso) is intellectual (3/0), while the plan to avoid detection by falling 'flat' is spoken very quietly (0/1), perhaps as if not to give himself away

The Tempest

Ferdinand

There be some Sports are painfull ; & their labor
3.1.1–15

Background: to test Ferdinand and Miranda's strength of affection for each other, Prospero has forced him, a prince unused to manual labour, to tidy up the wood that Caliban has brought. As such the speech is self-explanatory.

Style: solo

Where: near to Prospero's cell

To Whom: direct audience address

# of Lines: 16

Probable Timing: 0.50 minutes

Take Note: Within the onrushed F #1, the four pieces of major punctuation in the first four lines and the four extra breath-thoughts that quickly follow all seem to mark just where Ferdinand's (probable) handling the first menial task in his life requires extra effort, with the semicoloned moments perhaps requiring more effort than the others.

Ferdinand

1   There be some sports are painful, & their labor
    Delight in them [sets] off ; some kinds of baseness
    Are nobly undergone; and most poor matters
    Point to rich ends .

2   This my mean task
    Would be as heavy to me as odious, but
    The mistress which I serve quickens what's dead,
    And makes my labors pleasures .

3   O, she is
    Ten times more gentle [than] her father's crabbed ;
    And he's compos'd of harshness .

4   I must remove
    Some thousands of these logs, and pile them up,
    Upon a sore injunction .

5   My sweet mistress
    Weeps when she sees me work, & says such baseness
    Had never like executor .

6   I forget ;
    But these sweet thoughts, do even refresh my labors,
    Most [busil'est] when I do it .

Ferdinand

1   There be some Sports are painfull ; & their labor
     Delight in them [set] off : Some kindes of basenesse
     Are nobly undergon ; and most poore matters
     Point to rich ends : this my meane Taske
     Would be as heavy to me, as odious, but
     The Mistris which I serve, quickens what's dead,
     And makes my labours, pleasures : O She is
     Ten times more gentle, [then] her Father's crabbed ;
     And he's compos'd of harshnesse .

2   I must remove
     Some thousands of these Logs, and pile them up,
     Upon a sore injunction ; my sweet Mistris
     Weepes when she sees me worke, & saies, such basenes
     Had never like Executor : I forget :
     But these sweet thoughts, doe even refresh my labours,
     Most [busie lest], when I doe it .

- and the occasional small cluster of unembellished words in the somewhat emotional (2/4) first three and half lines (' ; & their labor/
  Delight in them sets off :'; 'Are nobly undergon'; 'Point to rich ends';
  'Would be as heavy to me, as odious'; 'quickens what's dead') could
  well suggest a moment of rest before beginning the physical heavy
  work once again

- it's possible that he stops the work to condemn 'this my meane Taske'
  making his 'labours, pleasures', for these next three lines are not in-
  terrupted by major punctuation and are also passionate (2/3)

- then the comparison of Miranda ('ten times more gentle') to her father ('crabbed') is intellectual (3/1, F#1's last two lines), and highlighted by being set as emotional (semicolon created) surround
  phrases

- the relative care of F #2's first two lines (1/0) and the subject matter
  suggest that Ferdinand may have started his labours once more

- however, recalling his 'Mistris' tears and words move him to passion
  once more (2/2), and in finishing with the fact that he can 'refresh'
  himself from 'these sweet thoughts', so he becomes totally emotional
  (0/3 the last two lines of the speech)

BIBLIOGRAPHY

The most easily accessible general information is to be found under the citations of *Campbell,* and of *Halliday.* The finest summation of matters academic is to be found within the all-encompassing *A Textual Companion,* listed below in the first part of the bibliography under *Wells, Stanley and Taylor, Gary* (eds.)

Individual modem editions consulted are listed below under the separate headings 'The Complete Works in Compendium Format' and 'The Complete Works in Separate Individual Volumes,' from which the modem text audition speeches have been collated and compiled.

All modem act, scene, and/or line numbers refer the reader to *The Riverside Shakespeare,* in my opinion still the best of the complete works, despite the excellent compendiums that have been published since.

The F/Q material is taken from a variety of already published sources, including not only all the texts listed in the 'Photostatted Reproductions in Compendium Format' below, but also earlier individually printed volumes, such as the twentieth century editions published under the collective title *The Facsimiles of Plays from The First Folio of Shakespeare* by Faber & Gwyer, and the nineteenth century editions published on behalf of The New Shakespere Society.

The heading 'Single Volumes of Special Interest' is offered to newcomers to Shakespeare in the hope that the books may add useful knowledge about the background and craft of this most fascinating of theatrical figures.

PHOTOSTATTED REPRODUCTIONS OF THE ORIGINAL TEXTS IN COMPENDIUM FORMAT

Allen, M.J.B. and K. Muir, (eds.). *Shakespeare's Plays in Quarto.* Berkeley: University of California Press, 1981.

Blaney, Peter (ed.). *The Norton Facsimile (The First Folio of Shakespeare).* New York: W.W.Norton & Co., Inc., 1996 (see also Hinman, below).

Brewer D.S. (ed.). *Mr. William Shakespeare's Comedies, Histories & Tragedies, The Second/Third/Fourth Folio Reproduced in Facsimile.* (3 vols.), 1983.

Hinman, Charlton (ed.). *The Norton Facsimile (The First Folio of Shakespeare).* New York: W.W.Norton & Company, Inc., 1968.

Kokeritz, Helge (ed.). *Mr. William Shakespeare 's Comedies, Histories & Tragedies.* New Haven: Yale University Press, 1954.

Moston, Doug (ed.). *Mr. William Shakespeare's Comedies, Histories, and Tragedies.* New York: Routledge, 1998.

MODERN TYPE VERSION OF THE FIRST FOLIO IN COMPENDIUM FORMAT

Freeman, Neil. (ed.). *The Applause First Folio of Shakespeare in Modern Type.* New York & London: Applause Books, 2001.

MODERN TEXT VERSIONS OF THE COMPLETE WORKS IN COMPENDIUM FORMAT

Craig, H. and D. Bevington (eds.). *The Complete Works of Shakespeare.* Glenview: Scott, Foresman and Company, 1973.

Evans, G.B. (ed.). *The Riverside Shakespeare.* Boston: Houghton Mifflin Company, 1974.

Wells, Stanley and Gary Taylor (eds.). *The Oxford Shakespeare, William Shakespeare , the Complete Works, Original Spelling Edition,* Oxford: The Clarendon Press, 1986.

Wells, Stanley and Gary Taylor (eds.). *The Oxford Shakespeare, William Shakespeare, The Complete Works, Modern Spelling Edition.* Oxford: The Clarendon Press, 1986.

MODERN TEXT VERSIONS OF THE COMPLETE WORKS IN SEPARATE INDIVIDUAL VOLUMES

The Arden Shakespeare. London: Methuen & Co. Ltd., Various dates, editions, and editors .

Folio Texts. Freeman, Neil H. M. (ed.) Applause First Folio Editions, 1997, and following.

The New Cambridge Shakespeare. Cambridge: Cambridge University Press. Various dates, editions, and editors.

New Variorum Editions of Shakespeare. Furness, Horace Howard (original editor.). New York: 1880, Various reprints. All these volumes have been in a state of re-editing and reprinting since they first appeared in 1880. Various dates, editions, and editors.

The Oxford Shakespeare. Wells, Stanley (general editor). Oxford: Oxford University Press, Various dates and editors.

The New Penguin Shakespeare . Harmondsworth, Middlesex: Penguin Books, Various dates and editors.

The Shakespeare Globe Acting Edition. Tucker, Patrick and Holden, Michael. (eds.). London: M.H.Publications, Various dates.

SINGLE VOLUMES OF SPECIAL INTEREST

Baldwin, T.W. *William Shakespeare's Petty School.* 1943.

Baldwin, T.W. *William Shakespeare's Small wtin and Lesse Greeke.* (2 vols.) 1944.

Barton, John. *Playing Shakespeare.* 1984.

Beckerman, Bernard. *Shakespeare at the Globe, I 599-1609.* 1962. Berryman, John. *Berryman 's Shakespeare.* 1999.

Bloom, Harold. *Shakespeare: The Invention of the Human.* 1998. Booth, Stephen (ed.). *Shakespeare's Sonnets.* 1977.

Briggs, Katharine. *An Encyclopedia of Fairies.* 1976.

Campbell, Oscar James, and Edward G. Quinn (eds.). *The Reader's Encyclopedia of Shakespeare. 1966.*

Crystal, David, and Ben Crystal. *Shakespeare's Words: A Glossary & Language Companion.* 2002.

Flatter, Richard. *Shakespeare's Producing Hand.* 1948 (reprint).

Ford, Boris. (ed.). *The Age of Shakespeare.* 1955.

Freeman, Neil H.M. *Shakespeare's First Texts.* 1994.

Greg, W.W. *The Editorial Problem in Shakespeare: A Survey of the Foundations of the Text.* 1954 (3rd. edition).

Gurr, Andrew . *Playgoing in Shakespeare's London.* 1987. Gurr, Andrew. *The Shakespearean Stage, 1574-1642.* 1987. Halliday, F.E. *A Shakespeare Companion.* 1952.

Harbage, Alfred. *Shakespeare's Audience.* 1941.

Harrison, G.B. (ed.). *The Elizabethan Journals.* 1965 (revised, 2 vols.).

Harrison, G.B. (ed.). *A Jacobean Journal.* 1941.

Harrison, G.B. (ed.). *A Second Jacobean Journal.* 1958.

Hinman, Charlton. *The Printing and Proof Reading of the First Folio of Shakespeare.* 1963 (2 vols.).

Joseph, Bertram. *Acting Shakespeare.* 1960.

Joseph, Miriam (Sister). *Shakespeare's Use of The Arts of wnguage.*1947.

King, T.J. *Casting Shakespeare's Plays.* 1992.

Lee, Sidney and C.T. Onions. *Shakespeare's England : An Account Of The Life And Manners Of His Age.* (2 vols.) 1916.

Linklater, Kristin. *Freeing Shakespeare's Voice.* 1992.

Mahood, **M .M.** *Shakespeare's Wordplay.* 1957.

O'Connor, Gary. *William Shakespeare: A Popular Life.* 2000.

Ordish, T.F. *Early London Theatres.* 1894. (1971 reprint).

Rodenberg, Patsy. *Speaking Shakespeare.* 2002.

Schoenbaum. S. *William Shakespeare: A Documentary Life.* 1975.

Shapiro, Michael. *Children of the Revels.* 1977.

Simpson, Percy. *Shakespeare's Punctuation.* 1969 (reprint).

Smith, Irwin. *Shakespeare's Blackfriars Playhouse.* 1964.

Southern, Richard. *The Staging of Plays Before Shakespeare.* 1973.

Spevack, M. *A Complete and Systematic Concordance to the Works Of Shakespeare.* 1968-1980 (9vols.).

Tillyard, E.M.W. *The Elizabethan World Picture.* 1942.

Trevelyan, G.M. (ed.). *Illustrated English Social History.* 1942.

Vendler, Helen. *The Art of Shakespeare's Sonnets.* 1999.

Walker, Alice F. *Textual Problems of the First Folio.* 1953.

Walton, J.K. *The Quarto Copy of the First Folio.* 1971.

Warren, Michael. *William Shakespeare, The Parallel King Lear 1608-1623.*

Wells, Stanley and Taylor, Gary (eds.). *Modernising Shakespeare's Spelling, with Three Studies in The Text of Henry V.* 1975.

Wells, Stanley. *Re-Editing Shakespeare for the Modern Reader.* 1984.

Wells, Stanley and Gary Taylor (eds.). *William Shakespeare: A Textual Companion.* 1987.

Wright, George T. *Shakespeare's Metrical Art.* 1988.

HISTORICAL DOCUMENTS

Daniel, Samuel. *The Fowre Bookes of the Civile Warres Between The Howses Of Lancaster and Yorke.* 1595.

Holinshed, Raphael. *Chronicles of England, Scotland and Ireland.* 1587 (2nd. edition).

Halle, Edward. *The Union of the Two Noble and Illustre Famelies of Lancastre And Yorke.* 1548 (2nd. edition).

Henslowe, Philip: Foakes, R.A. and Rickert (eds.). *Henslowe's Diary.* 1961.

Plutarch: North, Sir Thomas (translation of a work in French prepared by Jacques Amyots). *The Lives of The Noble Grecians and Romanes.* 1579.

APPENDIX 1:
GUIDE TO THE EARLY TEXTS

A QUARTO (Q)

A single text, so called because of the book size resulting from a particular method of printing. Eighteen of Shakespeare's plays were published in this format by different publishers at various dates between 1594-1622, prior to the appearance of the 1623 Folio.

THE FIRST FOLIO (F1)'

Thirty-six of Shakespeare's plays (excluding *Pericles* and *Two Noble Kinsmen,* in which he had a hand) appeared in one volume, published in 1623. All books of this size were termed Folios, again because of the sheet size and printing method, hence this volume is referred to as the First Folio. For publishing details see Bibliography, 'Photostated Reproductions of the Original Texts.'

THE SECOND FOLIO (F2)

Scholars suggest that the Second Folio, dated 1632 but perhaps not published until 1640, has little authority, especially since it created hundreds of new problematic readings of its own. Nevertheless more than 800 modern text readings can be attributed to it. The **Third Folio** (1664) and the **Fourth Folio** (1685) have even less authority, and are rarely consulted except in cases of extreme difficulty.

APPENDIX 2:
WORD, WORDS, WORDS

PART ONE: VERBAL CONVENTIONS (AND HOW THEY WILL BE SET IN THE FOLIO TEXT)

"THEN" AND "THAN"

These two words, though their neutral vowels sound different to modern ears, were almost identical to Elizabethan speakers and readers, despite their different meanings. F and Q make little distinction between them, setting them interchangeably . The original setting will be used, and the modern reader should soon get used to substituting one for the other as necessary.

"I," "AY," AND "AYE"

F/Q often print the personal pronoun "I" and the word of agreement "aye" simply as "I." Again, the modern reader should quickly get used to this and make the substitution when necess ary. The reader should also be aware that very occasionally either word could be used and the phrase make perfect sense, even though different meanings would be implied.

"MY SELFE/HIM SELFE/HER SELFE" VERSUS "MYSELF/HIMSELF/HER-SELF"

Generally F/Q separate the two parts of the word, "my selfe" while most modern texts set the single word "myself." The difference is vital, based on Elizabethan philosophy. Elizabethans regarded themselves as composed of two parts, the corporeal "I," and the more spiritual part, the "self." Thus, when an Elizabethan character refers to "my selfe," he or she is often referring to what is to all intents and purposes a separate being, even if that being is a particular part of him- or herself. Thus soliloquies can be thought of as a debate between the "I" and "my selfe," and, in such speeches, even though there may be only one character on-stage, it's as if there were two distinct entities present.

UNUSUAL SPELLING OF REAL NAMES, BOTH OF PEOPLE AND PLACES

Real names, both of people and places, and foreign languages are often reworked for modern understanding. For example, the French town often set in Fl as "Callice" is usually reset as "Calais." F will be set as is.

NON-GRAMMATICAL USES OF VERBS IN BOTH TENSE AND APPLICATION

Modern texts 'correct' the occasional Elizabethan practice of setting a singular noun with plural verb (and vice versa), as well as the infrequent use of the past tense of a verb to describe a current situation. The F reading will be set as is, without annotation.

ALTERNATIVE SETTINGS OF A WORD WHERE DIFFERENT SPELLINGS MAINTAIN THE SAME MEANING

F/Q occasionally set what appears to modern eyes as an archaic spelling of a word for which there is a more common modern alternative, for example "murther" for murder , "burthen" for burden, "moe" for more, "vilde" for vile. Though some modern texts set the Fl (or alternative Q) setting, others modernise. Fl will be set as is with no annotation.

ALTERNATIVE SETTINGS OF A WORD WHERE DIFFERENT SPELLINGS SUGGEST DIFFERENT MEANINGS

Far more complicated is the situation where, while an Elizabethan could substitute one word formation for another and still imply the same thing, to modern eyes the substituted word has an entirely different meaning to the one it has replaced. The following is by no means an exclusive list of the more common dual-spelling, dual-meaning words

anticke-antique	mad-made	sprite-spirit
born-borne	metal-mettle	sun-sonne
hart-heart	mote-moth	travel-travaill
human-humane	pour-(po wre)-power	through-thorough
lest-least	reverent-reverend	troth-truth
lose-loose	right-rite	whether-whither

Some of these doubles offer a metrical problem too, for example "sprite," a one syllable word, versus "spirit." A potential problem occurs in *A Midsummer Nights Dream,* where the modern text s set Q1's "thorough," and thus the scansion pattern of elegant magic can be established, whereas F1's more plebeian "through" sets up a much more awkward and clumsy moment.

The F reading will be set in the Folio Text, as will the modern texts' substitution of a different word formation in the Modern Text. If the modern text substitution has the potential to alter the meaning (and sometimes scansion) of the line, it will be noted accordingly.

PART TWO: WORD FORMATIONS COUNTED AS EQUIVALENTS FOR THE FOLLOWING SPEECHES

Often the spelling differences between the original and modern texts are quite obvious, as with "she"/"shee". And sometimes Folio text passages are so flooded with longer (and sometimes shorter) spellings that, as described in the General Introduction, it would seem that vocally something unusual is taking place as the character speaks.

However, there are some words where the spelling differences are so marginal that they need not be explored any further. The following is by no mean s an exclusive list of word s that in the main will not be taken into account when discussing emotional moments in the various commentaries accompanying the audition speeches.

(modern text spelling shown first)

and- &	murder - murther	tabor - taber
apparent - apparant	mutinous - mutenous	ta'en - tane
briars - briers	naught - nought	then - than
choice - choise	obey - obay	theater - theatre
defense - defence	o'er - o're	uncurrant - uncurrent
debtor - debter	offense - offence	than - then
enchant - inchant	quaint - queint	venomous - venemous
endurance - indurance	reside - recide	virtue - vertue
ere - e'er	Saint - S.	weight - waight
expense - expence	sense - sence	
has - ha's	sepulchre - sepulcher	
heinous - hainous	show - shew	
I'll - Ile	solicitor - soliciter	
increase - encrease	sugar - suger	

APPENDIX 3:
THE PATTERN OF MAGIC, RITUAL &
INCANTATION

THE PATTERNS OF "NORMAL" CONVERSATION

The normal pattern of a regular Shakespearean verse line is akin to five pairs of human heart beats, with ten syllables being arranged in five pairs of beats, each pair alternating a pattern of a weak stress followed by a strong stress. Thus, a normal ten syllable heartbeat line (with the emphasis on the capitalised words) would read as

weak- STRONG, weak - STRONG, weak- STRONG, weak- STRONG, weak- STRONG
(shall I com- PARE thee TO a SUMM- ers DAY)

Breaks would either be in length (under or over ten syllables) or in rhythm (any combinations of stresses other than the five pairs of weak-strong as shown above), or both together.

THE PATTERNS OF MAGIC, RITUAL, AND INCANTATION

Whenever magic is used in the Shakespeare plays the form of the spoken verse changes markedly in two ways . The length is usually reduced from ten to just seven syllables, and the pattern of stresses is completely reversed, as if the heartbeat was being forced either by the circumstances of the scene or by the need of the speaker to completely change direction. Thus in comparison to the normal line shown above, or even the occasional minor break, the more tortured and even dangerous magic or ritual line would read as

STRONG - weak, STRONG- weak, STRONG - weak, STRONG
(WHEN shall WE three MEET a GAINE)

The strain would be even more severely felt in an extended passage, as when the three weyward Sisters begin the potion that will fetch Macbeth to them. Again, the spoken emphasis is on the capitalised words and the effort of, and/or fixed determination in, speaking can clearly be felt.

> THRICE the BRINDed CAT hath MEW"D
> THRICE and ONCE the HEDGE-Pigge WHIN"D
> HARPier CRIES, 'tis TIME, 'tis TIME.

UNUSUAL ASPECTS OF MAGIC

It's not always easy for the characters to maintain it. And the magic doesn't always come when the character expects it. What is even more interesting is that while the pattern is found a lot in the Comedies, it is usually in much gentler situations, often in songs *(Two Gentlemen of Verona, Merry Wives of Windsor, Much Ado About Nothing, Twelfth Night, The Winters Tale)* and/or simplistic poetry *(Loves Labours Lost* and *As You Like It),* as well as the casket sequence in *The Merchant of Venice.*

It's too easy to dismiss these settings as inferior poetry known as doggerel. But this may be doing the moment and the character a great disservice. The language may be simplistic, but the passion and the magical/ritual intent behind it is wonderfully sincere. It's not just a matter of magic for the sake of magic, as with Pucke and Oberon enchanting mortals and Titania. It's a matter of the human heart's desires too. Orlando, in *As You Like It,* when writing peons of praise to Rosalind suggesting that she is composed of the best parts of the mythical heroines because

> THEREfore HEAVen NATure CHARG"D
> THAT one B0Die SHOULD be FILL'D
> WITH all GRACes WIDE enLARG"D

And what could be better than Autolycus *(The Winters Tale)* using magic in his opening song as an extra enticement to trap the unwary into buying all his peddler's goods, ballads, and trinkets.

To help the reader, most magic/ritual lines will be bolded in the Folio text version of the speeches.

ACKNOWLEDGMENTS

Neil dedicated *The Applause First Folio in Modern Type*
"To All Who Have Gone Before"
and there are so many who have gone before in the sharing of Shakespeare through publication. Back to John Heminge and Henry Condell who published *Mr. William Shakespeares Comedies, Histories, & Tragedies* which we now know as The First Folio and so preserved 18 plays of Shakespeare which might otherwise have been lost. As they wrote in their note "To the great Variety of Readers.":

> Reade him, therefore; and againe, and againe : And if then you doe not like him, surely you are in some manifest danger, not to understand him. And so we leave you to other of his Friends, whom if you need, can be your guides: if you neede them not, you can lead yourselves, and others, and such readers we wish him.

I want to thank John Cerullo for believing in these books and helping to spread Neil's vision. I want to thank Rachel Reiss for her invaluable advice and assistance. I want to thank my wife, Maren and my family for giving me support, but above all I want to thank Julie Stockton, Neil's widow, who was able to retrive Neil's files from his old non-internet connected Mac, without which these books would not be possible. Thank you Julie.

Shakespeare for Everyone!

Paul Sugarman, April 2021

AUTHOR BIOS

Neil Freeman (1941-2015) trained as an actor at the Bristol Old Vic Theatre School. In the world of professional Shakespeare he acted in fourteen of the plays, directed twenty-four, and coached them all many times over.

His groundbreaking work in using the first printings of the Shakespeare texts in performance, on the rehearsal floor and in the classroom led to lectures at the Shakespeare Association of America and workshops at both the ATHE and VASTA, and grants/fellowships from the National Endowment for the Arts (USA), The Social Science and Humanities Research Council (Canada), and York University in Toronto. He prepared and annotated the thirty-six individual Applause First Folio editions of Shakespeare's plays and the complete *The Applause First Folio of Shakespeare in Modern Type*. For Applause he also compiled *Once More Unto the Speech, Dear Friends*, three volumes (Comedy, History and Tragedy) of Shakespeare speeches with commentary and insights to inform audition preparation.

He was Professor Emeritus in the Department of Theatre, Film and Creative Writing at the University of British Columbia, and dramaturg with The Savage God project, both in Vancouver, Canada. He also taught regularly at the National Theatre School of Canada, Concordia University, Brigham Young University.. He had a Founder's Ring (and the position of Master Teacher) with Shakespeare & Company in Lenox, Mass: he was associated with the Will Geer Theatre in Los Angeles; Bard on the Beach in Vancouver; Repercussion Theatre in Montreal; and worked with the Stratford Festival, Canada, and Shakespeare Santa Cruz.

Paul Sugarman is an actor, editor, writer, and teacher of Shakespeare. He is founder of the Instant Shakespeare Company, which has presented annual readings of all of Shakespeare's plays in New York City for over twenty years. For Applause Theatre & Cinema Books, he edited John Russell Brown's publication of *Shakescenes: Shakespeare for Two* and The Applause Shakespeare Library, as well as Neil Freeman's Applause First Folio Editions and *The Applause First Folio of Shakespeare in Modern Type*. He has published pocket editions of all of Shakespeare's plays using the original settings of the First Folio in modern type for Puck Press. Sugarman studied with Kristin Linklater and Tina Packer at Shakespeare & Company where he met Neil Freeman.